THE SPIRITUAL
CURRENCY

DONALD THOMPKINS

NEITH PUBLISHING

Contents

Foreword

If you are like me was raised by the church and it's doctrines depending on what religious background you were associated with. We were taught about some of the different passages they talked about money, tithes, and taxes. Have you ever wondered just how the financial systems came into existence? We've been taught the modern financial day systems through modern day teachings. Have you ever wondered how did it get to this global stature? This book takes you into the history of how currency became. It connects the spiritual and the physical. I asked that you read this with an open mind free from your indoctrinated mind of Sophist theologians seeking to exploit hard working people with spiritually franchise monetary doctrine. Will it test your beliefs? NO, but will give you the historic genesis of these beliefs YES! Will it challenge your thinking? It absolutely will. Will it make you want to research and dig deeper it absolutely will. You will find everything you need to dig deeper the references from outstanding scholars are at your fingertips. Mr. Thompkins has put together a well thought out and informational piece of literature. You're in for a real literary experience in both history and spiritual revelations. I learned so much in reading this book. It opened me up into exploring Roman, British, and American History dating back to the early centuries. Take your time and enjoy this read.

Patricia Henderson

CHAPTER ONE

THE SPIRITUAL ECONOMY

A ncient Temples, often overlooked in their historical significance, were not just places of worship but also the precursors
to modern-day banks (Thirty Thousand Gods before Jehovah, P.67).
The underlying theory was that all blessings originated from a
divine source. This unique arrangement, where the empire's gold
and wealth were housed in the sacred temple's abode, was a
testament to the power of spirituality and a strategic move to
protect the nation's wealth. It's a fascinating insight into the early
stages of the evolution of spirituality and religion, inviting you to
delve deeper into this intriguing history. My primary objective is to
shed light on the enduring nature of spirituality, which predates
the very concept of religion by millennia. At its core, religion can
be viewed as a commercialized form of spirituality, a transition
I aim to depict vividly. This shift from a personal and spiritual
connection to a more structured and commercialized system is a
pivotal aspect of our exploration. I urge you to be patient as we
delve into these ideas, all underpinned by a robust hypothesis,
inviting you to question and explore the intriguing evolution of
these concepts.

Remember that money has always been foreign to spirituality, as
indicated by the bible's example of Jesus running off the money
counters in the temple.

Under the realm of spirituality, sacrifices were made for what we
now interpret as 'sin'. ' It's crucial to understand that the concept of
sin, a term from the Christian era, refers to an imbalance. Therefore, an animal sacrifice of various types and quantities would be
offered to a God based on your request and culture. This wouldn't
always occur due to some form of imbalance. (I will be using sin,
but in terms of imbalance. Furthermore, the book will alter our
modern understanding of the word sin.) Often, sacrifices may have
been made as a gift or contribution to a God for his/her assis-
tance with requests made and thanks, challenging our traditional

understanding of this term and opening new, thought-provoking perspectives.

One thing to bear in mind, whether you are studying ancient spirituality or any form of religion: There is always a cost associated with interacting with the Gods or gods of ancient times or modern-day religions. I'm asking that the reader be patient with me on the use of the word God and gods out of the tradition of religious understanding that you may worship. It is for a good reason, so it will be indisputably clear that the transformation of spirituality to religion and how the monetization process in religion gave birth to what became state-sponsored religion. Remember that any interaction between God and the gods is spiritual or religious.

There is a cost associated with worship. Even if it was you being thankful to your deity, you are still giving an energy of thanks paid from you toward that deity, a significant exchange in the realm of spirituality and a reminder of the profound responsibilities that come with such interactions.

Now, let's establish the basis of understanding to assist with this concept of enlightenment. We will use three numbers as a basis. We will now use spiritual and religious philosophy to explain these numbers of 123. The meaning of these numbers will be as the ancient Egyptian philosophy expressed numbers as quantitative and qualitative, but all in terms of steps in creation leading to manifestation. (A Study of Numbers. P. 29 – 30)

In every spirituality or religion, even baking a cake. You are going to start with steps . Step 1, Step 2, and Step 3. Creation leading to manifestation is no different. Let's use the ancient Egyptian Trinity as an example of spirituality. Most may be familiar with the names, even if not the philosophy. Then, we will discuss the idea of the religious trinity.

Ancient Egyptian Trinity.
Matriarchy.
Mother and Son: Spiritual, Mystical, Esoteric, Private.
Soul   Step 1 = Father/Osiris
Spirit   Step 2 = Mother/ Isis
Body   Step 3 = Son/ Horus

Original Religious Trinity.
Matriarchy.
Mother and Son: Spiritual. Mystical, Esoteric, Private.
Soul   Step 1 = Father
Spirit Step 2 = Mother

Body Step 3 = Son

Christian Trinity
Patriarchy.
Father and Son: Physical. Materialistic, Public, Secular.
Soul   Step 1 = Father
Body Step 2 = Son
Spirit Step 3 = Holy Ghost
The Holy Spirit took the place of the mother in the Christian Trinity. Under the patriarch system, the Holy Spirit reduced the power of the matriarchy to reduce the woman to the state of a vessel or property.

As I stated before, 123 is the point of reference for a significant part of this system, which will become the buttress of the religious system. It will be copied but interpreted from the spiritual metaphor into the literal and physical.

The ancient temples served as the community centers of their state; however, they are still based on the natural law of creation, as shown in the examples of 123.

Egyptian Temples.

    1. Heliopolis: The seat of God.; instructions from God heard.

    2. Memphis.: Written law received from Heliopolis (God) executed by the government/kingdom and municipalities.

    3. Thebes: These are received here for implementation and communication with the population. (The spiritual technology of ancient Egypt.)

These were the city's three main temples, which handled the Kingdom's structure. They served as universities of learning, spiritual centers of worship, banks, and courts. The laws were based on spirituality.

I stated earlier on in this book about the spiritual process of communicating with God or the gods. There will always be some form of cost based on your needs. The high priests and temple bodies address the care of the deities and dealt with the spiritual needs of the people. The people choose their deity based on their life, needs, and focus. But you address the relationship with your God or gods. Your sacrifice was on you. They just guided you. Remember these things as you continue to read: Your relationship with your God or gods was based on a direct relationship. There was no mediator between you and your deity or God. You had a spiritual connection to your God or deity that was direct with no need for a mediating type of figure. To paint a picture of how religion took spirituality out of spirituality and made it physical in the text literally.

I plan to show you how the Christian system created our current-day monetary system. Even how they created law in the church that became the law of the land in the Western world based on the ancient system I already expressed. I plan to show you dates on a timeline before, during, and after Jesus. Western religion took over Europe and began to export its system of government, commerce, and law, all under their religious/charter. The eventual corporate structure, the earliest stated government idea, duplicated the latter. Operating under its **"Auctoritas Ecclesie"** (Promissory *notes on the treasury of merits*.) The so-called spiritual but actual religious authority created puppet kings and queens. Divine rights claim numerous edicts from the 1st century CE, then the Magna Carta laid the basis for ecclesiastical feudalistic secular laws. The deadliest to the world community. The Edict of Demarcation gave birth to the doctrine of Discovery placed in the world and trust beginning charter, later to be named corporations. Starting with the oldest forms of charter. (Here we go, remember?) 1,2,3 temple in the Major cities. This reflects my hypothesis about these cities—The Vatican, London and Washington DC have an obelisk structure, and the Vatican and London obelisk came from Egypt. This reflects manifestation following Steps 1, 2, And 3.

CHAPTER TWO

SPIRITUAL CURRENCY TURNED ACUTE MATERIALISM

I want to argue that before the Greco-Roman era of circa 6th century BCE, in the 5th Century CE, Rome, as a Republic, became an empire when Octavia turned Emperor Augustus. (Wikipedia) what would become the Greek Empire was a Mediterranean construct and evolved from it, not because of it. (Dr. John Henrik Clark.) I declare that what would become of a Greek empire was part of an Egyptian Greco influence. The Septuagint was translated from Hebrew by Jews in Greece at the request of Ptolemy II of Egypt. I would be remiss not to mention that Martin Luther took issue with this Hellenistic interpretation of the Septuagint. Luther suggested that the interpreters did not have an exact knowledge of Hebrew and that their version was as void of meaning as harmony. (The Hebraic Tongue Restored Vol.1-2. P. 24). There were several suggestions that maybe the Septuagint had another translation added of Esdras; and that this version was sent to Jerusalem for approval as a paraphrase. The Sanhedrin granted their demand as this tribunal comprised seventy judges in confirmation of the law. The version received the name of the Septuagint version, which is to say it was approved by Seventy. (The Hebraic Tongue Restored Vol. 1-2. P. 44)

The Hebrew language was a direct result of the Egyptian hieroglyphic languages (Here we go, Step 1, Step 2, & Step 3), which featured three forms of language. Hieroglyphic, heretic, and demotic. Hieroglyphic: God's language or word; Heretic.: kings and business language. And Demotic.: the commoners or Ebonics of the language. I would be remiss not to point out the architect of Judaism, Moses, a product of the Egyptian mystery spiritual system. He also wrote in a three-dimensional manner that reflected his priestly sacerdotal education. (The Hebraic Tongue Restored. View the Forward.) A Persian Greco argument of influence can be suggested based on two separate invasions of Greek city-states by Darius and Xerxes in the 5th century BCE. Aristotle even claimed that the Magi were more ancient than the Egyptians, claiming that Zoroastrianism was six millennia older than Plato. It is also essential to add that after the invasion of Xerxes, he left behind Ostanes (Persian Hushtana.), a Persian saga to teach Magian ideas in Greece. (Original Magic: The rituals and initiation of the Persian Magi. P. 10-11) Pliny the Elder pointed to additional Greek minds like Pythagoras, Empedocles, and Democritus, having traveled to study the science of Zoroaster. (Original Magic. pg10)

I stated above that the Greek city-states that would become empires resulted from the Mediterranean gestation of thousands of years of knowledge. I believe I have laid the foundation of my understanding. However, I would like to elaborate on this by pointing out that these Greek men of wisdom were not only familiar with ancient Persian knowledge of spirituality but also with science created by the invasion of Darius and Xerxes. Cyrus the Great did invade Egypt, causing the Egyptian Mystery Systems to open their doors to said Greek philosophers. (Original Magic.) The Magi would become commonplace within the region and known as spiritual authorities and educators. However, the favor of the invasion would be returned under King Philip, the second of Macedonia's son, known to history as Alexander the Great.

Alexander the Great conquered land from Greece to India. (Wiki) The largest empire in history. Aristotle tutored Alexander at the age of 13. (Stolen Legacy) Aristotle's reference to the Persians and Egyptians shows that he was very familiar with these two ancient resources: Sage, a rich reservoir of spiritual and cultural science, an empire that sustains knowledge centers around the world. Not to mention, physical gold and silver were kept in the temples. He added India, Tibet, and more through this process of conquering, creating a mighty sage buttress of all the ancient world's tens of thousands of years, records, wisdom, and treasuries. To give birth to the knowledge Jambalaya is called Hellenistic culture.

The Hellenistic period was the cheat code to human spiritual DNA because it was the perfect blend or mixture of every school of interest in the ancient, civilized, and known world. A globally known civilized recipe of rebranded ancient knowledge called the Hellenistic period served from a metaphoric pot, which I will call the Hellenistic cultural Jambalaya. (Wiki)

The ingredients are Olympicism/ Hellenism, Babylonian spirituality, Hellenistic Judaism, Zoroastrianism, Hinduism, and Buddhism. The recipe comes in Greek, Persian, Aramaic, and Indo-Aryan. For the record, and the purpose of being accurate, Hellenistic Culture is Greco-Buddhism, Hellenistic culture, and Buddhism. (Wiki)

We must acknowledge that the Greeks were not very kind to some of its great philosophers: executions, mob attacks, murders, exiling, and destroying property, as well as schools. (Stolen Legacy) Only certain forms of philosophy were accepted, the most widely accepted philosophies of Stoicism, Epicureanism, and Pyrrhonism. These three philosophies were influenced by India, Babylonian/ Persian, and various forms of Buddhism.

It also became clear that Egyptian and Persian Greco spirituality was dangerous concerning a spiritual-based philosophy in Greece, more so for the former than the latter. However, a Greco-Egyptian or Greco-Persian twist was palatable.

Spiritualism, right-brain idealism, which was Egyptian, was rejected—the Babylonian, Greco-Persian version of physicalism/ tangibleness.

Egyptian Spirituality

Isft :(Isfet), Wrongdoing, falsehood = burden unbalanced.

Answer.: to become or return to balance.

Greco-Persian. (Sumerian- Babylonian/Persian.)

Sin: Wrongdoing, Evil, and Falsehood = Debt.

Answer: Pay the (By physical means.) Debt = Money, offering. Physical labor.

Unable to pay the debt or charge = slavery for the debt or becoming property.

Cheikh Anta Diop: The Greeks did not view the gods in the same light as the Egyptians and "reduced them to the level of men." (The spiritual technology of ancient Egypt. P. 195)

Pliny The Elder: A priest of Arabia placed a tithe on the incense trade. (30,000 Gods before Jehovah.P.60)

I Samuel. 2:13

This particular verse gives an example of the ancient priesthood and how they would take what could be considered a percentage of the offerings that the people would bring to the temple for various reasons, including offerings and tithings, and partake in them themselves—in retrospect, living off of the hard work, sweat, and offerings of the people in the name of their God or gods.

TITHE:

NOUN

One-tenth of annual produce or earnings is formally taken as a TAX for the support of the Church and clergy.

Verb.

Pay or give as a tithe.

"He tithes 10 percent of his income to the church." (Oxford Languages.)

We have entertained some ancient world spiritual views based on multiple civilizations. We know that each culture did not see all deities in a spiritual sense but in a physical one and took exception to a divine intervention concept.

I want to introduce you to a form of our modern-day social construct and hierarchy that was refined for the Western World and has touched so much of the rest.

This social construct was built to feed the machine via the vehicle of all in God's name. It used a secular arrangement through a doctrine of the divine right that created a hierarchy that self-created itself based on the self-interest of one class over another. This genesis of our modern-day social construct of classism is called the Ancient Rome class system, which expresses itself in our society today for the sake of time and be-labor the point. Let's make this as simple as possible. There were (Here we go, Step 1, Step 2, and Step 3.) Three social classes in Rome. (Study.com)

Patrician Class: Aristocratic Families, Nobles, and the upper government hierarchy.

Plebeian Class: Working class people or middle class.

Slave Class: Enslaved people or freedmen.

The Conflict of The Orders (497 – 287 B.C.E) (STUDY.COM)

The (Roman conflict was a political fight between the Patricians & Plebeians classes) the conflict created a more elaborate structure that started to give protection and favor via law to specific groups under a word that has traveled down through millennia to reward and restrict us all depending on where the dice of life lands for you. The word is called "PRIVILEGE."

The Evolution of the (Patrician & Plebeian Conflict) Class List

1. Patricians and Plebeian.

2. Property based class. (Women were a part of that property-based system.)

3. Gender based class.

4. Enslave – Freedman class.

5. Non-Roman citizens.

Which would come to be defined as

FEUDALISM:

Noun

The dominant social system in medieval Europe, in which the nobility held lands from the crown in exchange for military service, and vessels were, in turn, tenants of the nobles, while the peasants (villeins or serfs) or obligated to live on their Lords land and give him homage, labor, and a share of the produce, notionally in exchange for military protection.

(Oxford Language.)

I want to state before we dive deeper into the subject. This book is not about religion and has no shape, form, or fashion. I am not looking to review anyone's religious beliefs or how they view God, gods, or deities in any fashion. I hope to have an open and honest discussion based on historical facts and give my overview as I see them, but I am not suggesting that these will be the views of anyone outside of myself or my personal views. All I can do is hope that this can begin a conversation. It is to help us understand where we are on the map of global understanding of religious structures and their interaction with us in our everyday lives and what they contribute or do not contribute. In some cases, it is clear. As we begin to embark on this subject, Rome is a great place to start based on the trajectory of its influence on our lives today in so many parts of the world. And this is the buttress of what would produce what we understand today. The genesis of the overarching idea through The Conflict of Orders produced feudalism, as defined above, based on the legislation that was put forth that created multiple classes and distinguished with the establishment of the word privilege. This word privilege in law would mean that any exception given by law to any class or person is not questioned; or even be considered in the jurisdiction of a legal proceeding based on feudalism. It will be evident that another system is pointed to above. Even before the category of classes evolved, the labels of enslaved people and freedmen were consistent. I think it is essential to understand that the system of slavery existed well before Rome, and this was a concept that was adopted Overall, within this era of which would later be classified under the description of Europe. Through the different information and the multiple books, I have researched, there seems to be a consensus about the population's feelings and the hierarchical hierarchy of that day, even in Greece, toward anyone enslaved. Aristotle considered white enslaved people as things. The Romans also had compunctions against enslaved whites, who they too termed as" a thing" Or should I say "RES (RAS). (They were white, and they were slaves. P.7)

There would not have been much evolution of thought on slavery because it carried over to 1st century B.C.E. Rome, with some of Rome's most prestigious minds adding their voice to the disdain.

Philosopher Varro labeled white slaves as nothing more than "tools that happen to have voices." (Instrumenti vocale). (They were white, and they were slaves. P.7).

Cato The Elder: White slaves, when old or ill, should be discarded along with their worn-out farm implements. (They were white, and they were slaves. P.7).

This book will mention slavery; it's a susceptible subject for many people. It's based on the form of a futuristic government that was arranged within these ancient societies that needed labor. The ideology of slavery would become so as we continue to travel through the years and millennia throughout this book. It would be the basis of the economy that we're going to come to understand as the title of this book states: The Spiritual Economy as we will see, slavery has visited every branch of humanity, and everyone has been subjugated to commerce by the hierarchy but historically under the definition of prisoner of war. But that definition would be somewhat elusive through the ages and would evolve into just for commerce. Please be advised that this book is not to judge whether it was appropriate or inappropriate at any point throughout history. Any branch of humanity or race experienced enslavement. Slavery is only being discussed to make my hypothesis clear. All these different activities throughout history through the vehicle as defined by law but established through what I consider to be The Ecclesia Expression of an organization that led to the enterprise; and the Nicene Christian version of what the world has known as Christianity, which would be arranged in the form of enterprise, all to create what we now call franchises born out of the materialistic form of spirituality expressed secularly: a gestated version of a spiritual world duplicated in the secular world. In the form of states, but in the same pattern as what we see in enterprise.

CHAPTER THREE

JESUS AND THE MONEY CHANGERS

E *vil will stand for all that reduce the spiritual to the physical (The Spiritual Technology OF Ancient Egypt.)*

I want to start with Jesus and the money changers in the temple. (Matthew 21:12-14.)

Jesus entered the temple and proceeded to drive out all those who were buying and selling there. He overturned the money changers' tables and benches of those selling doves. He even quoted scripture from his day, stating that God's house was meant for prayer, not what it was being turned into. As he said., "A den of robbers." (Matthew 21:12-14).

Interestingly, the word bench is translated into banco (bank) in Italian. This would lead me to believe that the money changers and their benches of that day were nothing more than what we will call our modern-day bankers in the actual church selling doves. I believe this is why Jesus referred to a den of robbers. What I find so interesting about this particular scripture is that it indicates that the Son of God found it foreign. Even for that day. The day of the Pagan that people would be money changers with benches or bankers would transact business in the temple. Let us be clear: this is a perfect example that was used even before. The establishment of what we understand as Christianity based on historical records, the Son of God, Jesus, knew that there was something wrong with the secular, being directly involved with the spiritual world, he acted against it. It's important to note that all contracts and business transactions were kept and filed at the temples of their day. This was under the idea that God should look over all transactions, and all transactions would be recorded by God because all blessings came from God. (30,000 gods before Jehovah. P.60)

The wealthy businessmen of the bible always use nefarious and secular means to gain wealth. Abraham of the Abrahamic religions, the founder of the three major religions of Judaism, Christianity, and the Muslim Religions, was also a very tricky businessman. Abraham even used his wife to seduce very wealthy, well-established businessmen, and this deception was centered around her beauty and his means to manipulate that process.

At this time, the 1st century CE was a polytheistic culture like the Greeks before them. Christianity was foreign to Rome, and there was not even the word Bishop being used, at least for the first circa 150 CE. The term papacy wasn't even an idea for the first three centuries (Francis A Sullivan). It is safe to say that the Romans were very much a pagan community. Several pagan religions were being practiced. But the one most or best known around that time was Magna Mater "Cybele "The Great Mother (WIKI). I find this extremely interesting for a society dating back to the Greeks, a patriarchal society that looked at women's property owned by the patriarch of the family. Nevertheless, they featured the top pagan religion. The Great Mother. This has a Northern African ring to me.

Christianity didn't come into existence as a singular idea. It was born from a diverse beginning featuring Gnostic Christianity (which The Greeks worked hard to eradicate) and Pauline Christianity. Jewish Christianity: The Judaism of Jewish Christianity is credited for setting the foundation of the Abrahamic religions (Persian Jews, who were liberated from Babylon by the Persian army). After so many inconsistencies of paganism as well as numerous versions of Christianity out of North Africa that was well established within the Greco-Roman area overall. There was mass persecution of Christians that was going on that's well documented. The beginning of the end of this persecution of the Christians was established by Emperor Constantine. Emperor Constantine passed the edict called the Edict of Milan in 313 AD. Now, if my memory serves me correctly, the actual name of the actual mandate was the Edict of Tolerance.

This edict did not name Christianity or endorse Christianity as a state religion. This will come along much later. What this mandate did was it tolerated Christianity. Making Christianity legal, therefore eliminating the persecution of Christian Christians at that time. Christianity was granted legal acceptance under the law of that time. What does Edict do as well? It restored all seized properties taken by the state from Christians who practice Christianity. (Wiki) However, I think it is imperative to add this known fact to the overall details of the Edict of Milan and the actual tolerance that was given to Christianity and who may have been at the root of this shift in religious practice by Emperor Constantine. Emperor

Constantine also extended an offer of tax-free status for all offerings & tithes received by those willing to teach that version of
Christianity. (John Henry Clark) This was a black man who was the
Pope of Rome at the time out of North Africa. This pope went by
the name of Pope Miltiades. This great man was elected the 37th
pope in 311 A.D. Until January 314, when he died of natural causes.
He was the first pope to be given an official residence. Emperor
Constantine's' wife gave him the luxurious Lateran Palace. This
pope convinced Emperor Constantine to return cemeteries and
churches that the government had taken. Under Pope Miltiades's
reign, the Roman Emperor was converted to Christianity. After this,
Emperor Constantine gave the freedom of worship to Christians.
Pope Miltiades brought the final victory of the Christian Church
over Rome. This pope was the reigning pope over the process
that gave us the Edict of Milan and all the protections it provided
for the Christian community. This pope was so great that Saint
Augustine referred to him as"An excellent man, a true son of peace,
and a father of Christians." (Blacks who died for Jesus. P. 21-22)

It is essential to point out the conception of the Roman Catholic
Church that would be established. It must be pointed out that
there were three North African Black Emperors of Rome, as well as
three black popes from Rome. I feel it's imperative to point this out
because it accurately indicates the time, and there was no concept
of colorism and class as we may know it in modern times. Speaking
of the enslavement of different members of the human family, it is
also imperative that this is pointed out as a cause for cheap labor.
The definition of Prisoner of war evolved into what would become
commerce, this idealism was created at some point, but not back
then. People were just looked at as part of these different classes
and not based on what part of the human family you belong to.
I would hypothesize that the whole overall or overarching idea
of specific members of particular factions of the human family
being identified was for the sole purpose of when that prisoner
of war under enslavement became for commerce and exploitation
by the government, which was facilitated by a particular form of
Christianity.

Emperor Constantine appeared to release pressure and give
acceptance to Christians and Christianity. It seems that others were
not as fortunate at that time. Approximately five to six years after
this extraordinary revelation for the Christian Church Emperor
Constantine, in 319 A.D. ruled that if an owner of a white enslaved
person whipped him and, as a result, caused death. He should not

be criminalized If that slave succumbs to his injuries, Stating," He should not stand in any criminal accusation if the slave dies, and all statutes of limitations and legal interpretations are hereby set aside." (They were white, and they were slaves. P.7) This statement by Emperor Constantine speaks to the view of that date and time that actual enslaved people were property. This had to be the exact accepted view of the population and recognized in established law. As stated by Emperor Constantine.

Emperor Constantine had a lot on his hands and managed a whole lot through war and trying to keep his empire together that would include an eastern and a western part of the Roman Empire. There are many opinions on the subject, seeing that Emperor Constantine was classified as a pagan and that he received enlightenment based on conquering and war activity, according to history's most common explanation. However, some skeptics wonder if the timing of Emperor Constantine's conversion to Christianity was based on a decision that needed to be made on the subject because it was tearing his empire or could threaten to tear it apart. I tend to lean toward the latter explanation of the two, and the histories that I have viewed and several of the research pieces that I have done illustrate that this had to be a legitimate concern. This is somewhat like what countries state today as a threat to national security. This assumed that fear would soon be realized because the emperor would face what history has titled the Schism of the 4th century. I believe that the Edict of Milan was the beginning of his answer to rectifying the storms he saw coming. The storms he saw coming would be encapsulated within several names, but not one name would stand to be more paramount than the name Arius.

I recall growing up and hearing that you knew you made it if you were a celebrity or some public office figure if you could be recognized by just one name. Names like Bono, Madonna, Prince, Ali, Michael (Jackson, Jordan), Obama, Mozart, Michelangelo, and Buddha. Krishna And Jesus.... Etc. This name is a name you can say around any religious historian or students of history having to do with the church or spiritualities involving the development of Christianity as one of the world's top religions. This name struck fear around the 4th century and the schism. Legend says that Emperor Constantine even invited this gentleman to a council before to relieve himself of the biggest threat to stability in his realm and once he heard of the plan, he escaped into exile again. Without further ado..... This gentlemen's name was" **ARIUS."**

Arius shows up around 310 AD. Arius was a black African man from North Africa. Arius shows up in a fashion consistent with the terror that his name would bring throughout the pages of history when he shows up at the Diocese of Alexandria in Egypt, and he brings an uproar. He claims that God the Eternal Father had created his Son from nothing before the creation of other things. He also claims Jesus was the first creature and he was divine as was God. Some would think that this is exceptionally blasphemous, and that would be enough to have someone excommunicated, which he was excommunicated repeatedly and maybe even burned at the stake. But in true Arius fashion, that was not enough. Arius had something else to say. Arius, looking to one-up himself, said that" Jesus was an illusion." That he was" not of the same substance as God, yet he was only the best of created beings." This appears to be an introduction to the powerful personality of Arius and the hundreds of years of influence he would have on the Catholic Church in what would become known as Arianism and Arian Christianity in what the world now calls current date Europe after his death. This indicated the schism of the 4th century and what had to be dealt with, with other personalities that were not nearly as influential as Arius but very effective. (Black who die for Jesus. P. 34-35)

The Bishop of Alexandria put Arius out of the church. This battle would go back and forth between Arius and the Bishop of Alexander, with the Bishop of Alexander excommunicating Arius several times and exiling him. The Orthodox Bishop of Alexander declared Arius's preaching heretical and sent him away again in 312AD. Arius was called to appeal before the Council of 100 bishops convened in Alexandria, and they confirmed the ruling of the Orthodox Bishop to separate Arius from the Church.

Nevertheless, Arius was a potent adversary with powerful political connections. Causing to approve Constantine in Rome. This delegation required a full investigation into the matter to send an investigator to the Bishop of Alexander. The results of this investigation caused one of the most considerable councils in the history of the Catholic Church. This council was called to be in place. The Council of Nicaea in 325AD. This council was huge, and they called all the bishops from the eastern part of the empire and the western part of the Roman Empire. Rome paid all expenses. This Council will be the council that created what I classify as the European Catholic Church version of Christianity. One of the most important events to come out of this council was the Nicene Creed.

This set the bar for the belief of the Catholic Church. everyone who became Catholic would have to submit to, and it is used around the world. Arius and his group did not fare very well at this Council. Arius and his followers were banished once again. But this did not stop Arius because his preaching went public, and he started to convert nuns and priests to his side. They were representing Arianism. The council condemned Arius's interpretation of the father-son relationship and declared it was heretic. Arius believed that the father and the son were of the same substance, and this went against the Nicene Creed.

In 351 AD, Emperor Constantine became the sole ruling emperor of Rome. This divided the development of Arianism into three parts. Each one of these parts would have different groups that were highly violent with each other. Just as violent as they were toward the Catholic Church. However, the overall point is that Arian Christianity or Arianism had a strong foothold in what would become known as Europe. The Visigoths and many Germanic tribes became Arians. The Vandals of Spain became staunch Arians, and they brought in The Burgundy. The Franks were even Arians. Before they broke away and became Catholic, The Franks started to notice the importance or the enterprising nature of the Catholic Church, and Clovis I saw it as profitable. I think Clovis I went after the Arians because he knew he could confiscate their property and grow his empire, which became very beneficial, which we'll see soon. Arius was significant for so many different reasons, but one of the many, and there's several of the results that came from him, was the Catholic Christological System, The Ecumenical Council, and the Nicene Creed. Arius gave birth to Christianity is a form of Arianism. It will be identified as Arianism. And, by the term of Arian Christianity. Arius would be murdered in 361AD, but his legacy will live on for millennia and his immediate impact. It would be a thorn in the Catholic Church's side for hundreds of years via the Germanic tribes and the Angles. Later, The Angles became known as the Anglo-Saxon. (Blacks who died for Jesus. P. 35 – 38)

The enslavement of the human family was an institution well before the establishment of the Catholic Church. It must be understood that the enslavement of human beings was very much a part of the whole of Europe before it was classified as Europe's experience. The Catholic Church did not interrupt the process but was very much a part of it and appeared to endorse it. In time, you will see there were actual edicts that spoke to the fact of the actual enslavement of different members of the human family recommended and instructed by the Catholic Church itself via Edicts. The Romans enslaved thousands of early white inhabitants from Great Britain when they were known as Angles. In time, history will refer to them as Anglo-Saxon. As a description of the English race. This distinction of race is not the first time it will be witnessed. In this book, you will hear about races again. I'm just referring to in reference to the European family by a very influential Catholic Church Bishop. In the 6th century, Pope Gregory I witnessed a blonde-haired, blue-eyed English boy awaiting sale In a slave market in Rome. Pope Gregory inquired about the boy's origin and was told he was one of the Angles. **Gregory replied," No Angli, sed Angeli" (Not Angles, but Angels")**

The Franks were Arians before becoming Catholic Franks, which led to the conquest of the Visigoths in South Gule that was purely based on, in my opinion, the enterprising opportunity that Clovis I explored when he became a Catholic Frank. The Catholic Franks created a vast white slave market. (They were white, and they were slaves. P.7)

"After Charlemagne's conquest of the Saxony, during which many Pagan Saxons were enslaved. He set up a network of parish churches to maintain the priest and the church. Those living in the parish were to donate a house and land, as well as male and female (Saxon) slaves to the church for every 120 people in the parish." (They were white, and they were slaves. P.7)

The Edict of Thessalonica was issued by Theodosius I, Gratian, And Valentinian II Circa February 381 CE. This edict, and not the ones before, made Nicene Christianity the state religion of the empire. This edict also condemned other creeds, like the Creeds of Arianism, and made their persecutions acceptable. This edict ordered the closing of Egyptian temples, which would help Nicene Christianity began to spread more rapidly by forcing and coloniz-ing other religions, spiritual sites, and land as a prerequisite for a secular military kind. (Stolen Legacy. P.46) (Study.com)

Let's talk about the forms of money that were established at that time and how they spilled over into our modern-day times, and that would be Bills of Exchange, better known as promissory notes. The Jews of Lombardi and other great Italian dealers in money who were in the Dark Ages, were among the ones in the third-century European banking system that were considered inventors of the Bills of Exchange or promissory notes. But let's be clear: this was a necessity. However, it is also known as the parent of schemes based on the danger of trying to transport money (Gold & Silver) or jewelry from point to point. These bills of exchange or promissory notes were used to collect your value at different places without a chance of being robbed but at a price. The name of the Lombardi was also referred to as Lombardi merchants. The name Lombardi is so sacred to money handlers and bankers that a street in London is named after them as the celebrated Cardinal Baronius inserted nearly three centuries in his ecclesiastical history. It has been abducted as proof that Bills of Exchange were employed as early as the 4th century. (The law of bills of exchange, promissory notes, checks, etc.1839. P.2)

The philosopher Synesius afterwards becoming Bishop of Ptolemais About 410AD. Having converted a pagan philosopher, Evagrius of Cyrene to Christianity. After being converted, Evagrius brought 300 pieces of gold to Synesius for the poor, and he required a bill under his hand that Christ should repay him in another world, and Synesius agreed to that arrangement. Evagrius not long afterward, feeling that death was upon him, he directed his people to ensure the bill was buried in the coffin with him. It is said that soon after his death, he appeared in a vision of his friend, the bishop and he told the bishop to come to his grave and take his bill. Synesius followed the instructions that his friend gave in the vision. He removed the bill from the hand of his friend's body. Still, he also discovered a receipt upon the Bill Stating," I, Evagrius the philosopher, salute thee, Most High Bishop Synesius. I have received the debt which is written in this paper with thine own handwriting. I was satisfied and have no lawful claim for gold with which I gave to thee and by thee to Christ, our God and Savior." (The Law of bills of exchange, promissory notes, checks, etcetera. 1839. P.2)

CHAPTER FOUR

ALL IN GOD'S NAME

Now, we are about to enter the Dark Ages. The Dark Ages are classified as between the 5th and 10th centuries AD. But some put it in between the 5th and the 15th century. (wiki) The Dark Ages was a very challenging time based on the war between the different groups in what is now called Europe. It should be clear at this point that Christianity has many versions. Still, most of the versions stemming from North Africa are starting to become a challenge for the new version of Christianity called Nicene Christianity. This Nicene Christianity was a rebranding of Christianity under Hellenistic Christian branding, representing several different ancient cultural spirituality but under the brand of materialism. Many schools of thought state that the hierarchy of kings and queens was illiterate during this time and could not read, which some would challenge (Stolen Legacy). Yet, based on some of the history that we're going to touch on and what appears to be the manipulation of edicts current day called contracts between the Paper See and these particular kingdoms would lead one to assume that maybe there were some forms of illiteracy with some of these kings because It appears that they were duped. We will start to see the power of the actual church, but up under bishops, and at some point, we will see the term aristocratic bishops. The Catholic Church would begin to bring all these different bishops up under its ecclesia's idea. Structured government in many places where there was actual structures of government would fall, the only source of governance within these particular city-states throughout Europe would be the different bishops that served in these areas. They often kept away different barbarians from invading and robbing the locals, and in different instances putting together groups including monks to go out and march against these barbaric groups to stave them off for the protection, of the actual community.

This statement alone, in the structure that was displaying itself, is a clear indication of the word that I introduced, I believe, in the first chapter talking about feudalism. We would find that as the Catholic Church spread its idea of ecclesia, it was also in hand with these different kings who wanted to use the actual stretch of this form of spirituality under the Nicene Creed. These different kings started to see the potential of the enterprise. As I've seen, the similarities between the Catholic Church and the ecclesia's agenda started to franchise these different spiritual sites under Arianism and several different forms of Christianity, bringing it up under the Catholic Church Ecclesia Scope. These kings saw this vehicle as very useful. They started to move throughout the process under the guidance of the pope, in many cases colonizing different areas under different European tribal structures, just as an off branch of the Hellenistic Greeks. Rome was a slave community. This was an essential part of its economic structure and the materialistic principle that it catered to, more so than the spiritual views of, let's say, the Egyptian Greco Philosophers of Greece, whose perspectives of ideology were rejected. We would see that the tribal structures that vary amongst the European groups would start to be relabeled as different races via one of the most—influential bishop from Ireland who came down into the Frankish Catholic Church, Bishop Columbanus. Through the description of the death defining of races instead of tribal communities, you also see the development of the racial component. Being used as a form of policy to achieve an objective, in my opinion, the furtherance of manipulation, divide and conquer tactics for not allowing another Conflict of The Order and a direct threat to the hierarchy and a now reformed Plebeian society that is a part of the aristocratic negotiated deal of privileges now protected by law. Patricia always had power by being part of the hierarchy. Still, now The Plebeian had skin in the game, and another class was created below them, which created a clear separation by the social construct of A FICTION made real by a contracted understanding of cooperation (between The Patricia & Plebeian) made real BY LAW. (Laws became a reflection of contracted agreements made PRIVILEGE representing monopoly & the states guaranteed protections in favor of commerce.) So now it was in their best interest to make sure there were no more additions based on the game, which was all about the property, property of land or people has admitted you into that Patrician group.

The Nicene Christianity became a very different description of spirituality than what was historically known prior to its creation. I must create some form of draft to show you how I believe the Catholic Church moved the description of spirituality into a secular realm. From my observation, an accounting system has been implemented to scale the spiritual and secular differences. So, within one's mind, you must envision a scale like balancing an account. To the left, you will have the spiritual, which represents assets. To the right, with a line dividing left from right, you will have the secular, representing liabilities. Decide to the left representing spiritual assets that would be classified as the private side. The side to the right representing secular liabilities would be the public side. As we go further within the book, you will see a debate in the early 12 to 15th century, where the papacy was required to define the two keys that Saint Peter gave over to the pope as the Vicar of Christ. (Promissory Notes on the Treasury of Merits. P.28-30) The debate would cover what God covers when it comes to forgiveness and what part is covered by man. Again, you have the separation of two, where you have the private and the public. Please remember that the spiritual, asset, and private sides are on the left side, and to the right, you will have the secular, liability, and public sides. With that thinking, the two keys represent one side, and one key represents the other side of the two keys that were supposed to be given to the Pope or the Catholic Church at Saint Peter's death. One of the keys would be on the left side. It would be on the left side with the spiritual, asset, and private, and the description of that key on that side would be ordered in that key of order. Is Sacerdotal controlled by and only by God? The right side, representing secular liabilities to the public, will be controlled by the key, which the papacy calls jurisdiction. So, the graph that I will attempt to put in place to help assist you with this theory will help clear the idea with this aid for the furtherance of the book when we get deeper into my theory based on a plethora of historical events.

As stated above, my theory is that the bar of spirituality has been moved from one point to another. The purpose of moving the bar from spirituality is to move it out of the description I gave you above, somewhat out of God's order. Where forgiveness is given by God and a debt can be associated with it. As stated above, the Key of Order is under God's control, and there cannot be any human or secular interference. So, by lowering the bar and moving it over where the layperson individual would think you're in spirituality when you're actually in the realm of the secular, which puts you under the jurisdiction of the Catholic Church. The theory is that the fall within the bible describes how man fell from being a spiritual being and fell into the flesh. The ancient description is that anything in the spirit is pure, but as soon as anything falls into matter or any form of body, that's the definition of evil, or, as we say today, sin. Based on the Sumerian culture, the Akkadian, the Babylonian, and then Persian, anything having to do with the physical (secular) or evil, there is a debt associated with it. The graph I intend to explain here will give you a visualization of what I'm stating. I hypothesize that the original forms of ancient spirituality are scaled from -5 through -1. The bar measuring spirituality was lowered to the buttress or basis of true spirituality. Still, the beginning of materialism on the scale with materialism beginning at 0 to 1 represents God or a divine presence but at the beginning of a material/physical existence. On that same scale, numbers 2 through 5 represent your saintly or high priest class. Making 6 through 10 secular or worldly existence, total materialism, and physical not of God.

-5 -4 -3 -2 -1
True Spirituality
The Father
The Father
0 (0 to 1) 1
Material
Spirituality
The Mother
The Son
2 3 4 5
Saintly
High Priest
The Son
The Holy Spirit
6 7 8 9 10
Total Materialism
Physical Debt Sin
Death/Slavery
Death/ Slavery
Sin &Physical Debt

Emperor Constantine and emperors who would follow via different edicts over time didn't instantly make everyone a Christian. Pagan worship was widespread and still affluent at that time, and for hundreds of years to come, Paganism was alive and plentiful.

The issue became the following: What was the exact definition of a Christian? What did or did not make you a Christian? What actions did you need to display to define yourself as a Christian? Did a Bishop in your city make your city Christian? The power of the bishops was immense. The edict of Emperor Constantine caused some confusion based on the reality of the edict, making Christianity tolerable and legal to express for the community. What was not apparent was the unforeseen disconnect between the bishops and the hierarchy from the later bishops or religious. Hierarchy that came along from the older ones that experienced torture and torment, and persecution for Christianity versus the ones that didn't. And just as stated before, there is a disconnect between the hierarchy. Then, the initial bishops were extremely poor, and the hierarchical bishops were extremely wealthy. (The Frankish Church. P.1)

It cannot be understated that the power of the bishops in these cities became immense. The barbarian presence within these communities was widespread throughout what would become Europe. It cannot be understated there were often problems with these barbarian groups invading cities, robbing, raping, pillaging, and several other things involved. The bishops in these cities were often the only thing between the people being violated, and these barbarian groups were the bishops who stood firm. Sometimes, they even LED resistance against these barbarian groups when secular authority failed. Their communities. These bishops had taken the place of secular Roman officials as local protectors and often negotiated different agreements that were favorable for the communities they were protecting and representing when negotiating with the barbarians. This developed a sacred trust of the community and the bishops beyond any secular authority or government structure that could or be developed. So, when these groups would come in, they always look to the bishops for leadership to try to control or rule over the group. There was no secular authority or king, independent of these very powerful bishops who developed corporate power and influence over their communities and sometimes regions. Will it have any sway over the people? The struggle of invasion in these cities put pressure on the bishops to side, in some cases, with the Roman Catholic Church. In their victory, they proved that this Catholic Church God was superior to other gods and would bring them victory and prosperity, but only in God's favor. By doing so, these bishops started to observe that the bigger the church, the more magnificent the church. The more considerable donations and legacies that could be built for themselves and the offerings that started to come in were not regular offerings, or small offerings as they were before they started to get offers of large swaths of land. The offerings were large, small, and all variations in between. But these offerings will be given of whatever size will be for the purpose of sin and the so-called price of the salvation of their souls. The offerings were so tremendous and taxing that it asked whether a man's first responsibility was his family or whether it was the church. (The Frankish Church)

At this point, donations became a challenge for the church. Based on the volume and the vast amounts of donations and land that the church was receiving, the church had to figure out how it would be able to deal with all the large quantities. Wealth accumulates in the representation of all these people in the community of all social standings, giving donations for the salvation of their souls. The philosophy preaches that all donations that were given are the return of God to God, what belongs to God already. This demand of pressure for constant giving and the church receiving was not just a problem for the church in terms of all the large amounts of wealth; it was also a burden on the community because of the constant tax by the church for these so-called sins and salvation of their soul, because of it. However, from my research, it appears that the idea, as I alluded to initially with the Lombardi and the creation of the bills of exchange, promissory notes from the Lombardi merchants, and the enormous amounts of land that were being acquired by the bishops. On behalf of the Catholic Church at this point, it would be a burden that would prove to be irresistible to the soon-to-be development of the secular branch, the Merovingians. Where the bishops were not secular at all and were supposed to represent the spiritual, the most significant benefit of profit appeared to be the fear of the population of constant invasion of the barbarian groups, which at this point are being classified as people under the different Christian beliefs of Arianism and other forms. We will start to note that whenever these attacks occur on communities or being made the bishops would relate that, under the direction of the Catholic Church, to alleged sin by the community that's causing these things and God allowing them, which will cause the people to give up more and more and more for the protection or favor of God. This Nicene version of Christianity became the most profitable aspect of social status in the communities at this point It became more profitable, lucrative, and influential to be a bishop than a civil servant. In some cases, most civil servants or people serving in the hierarchy positions were Christian for social status; there clearly became a difference only from the keen eye of knowing that this social status was more associated with the Catholic Church than the classic agenda versus the actual spiritual religion of Christianity and this prosperity will be social hierarchically beneficial as we will see as we continue to go through the book for the purpose of financial gain labeled under Nicene Christianity.

In the 5th century, you will start to see the formation of the actual church, which is beginning to build out. You will begin to see Gallic monks who were Polytheistic in nature start to adopt the Christian faith for the possibilities of commerce that it presents. The promise of business and the ability to live their aesthetic life was very alluring to these groups. The movement of monks started to really grow, but it appears as if the different church bishops or religious organizations worked hand in hand with these groups, where the Catholic Church appeared to start reaching out more and more to them and allowing them to see the possibility of enterprise through the actual Catholic faith. We know this throughout history, especially during the Hellenistic period and now (The Frankish Church P.7-8). Roman Greco area had most of the population, and as I stated before, during the Dark Ages, most of the hierarchy and royal families were illiterate. You can look back as far as the Sumerian, Chaldean, and Egyptian Mesopotamia regions with spirituality, your monks served as your judges, lawyers, bookkeepers, and educators and would become the chief legislators and orchestrators of written understanding.

Between the Catholic Church and all secular Monarchies Etcetera. (The law of bills of exchange, promissory notes, checks, etcetera, 1839. P.2). This group was able to read, write, and keep records when it came to commerce or any other form of municipal or government functions within the realm. These were the groups that always kept account of those things based on records. This is why these groups were more important than any other group, with the building of what became the Nicene brand of Christianity and, in my opinion, the very first examples of what would become a blueprint for franchises. The basis of the Roman Empire developed through the understanding using religion as a new agreement or version of Christianity that will be called the Roman Catholic Church. This would give birth to a secular body of government under the jurisdiction of the church by vehicle of the divine right, the rulership of kings and queens would be expressed initially through the Merovingian (long-haired) Kings.

As the 5th-century church settled in, it became a very rich one. And I hate to make it seem as if I'm overstating the issue, but I'm not. The church now owns great lands, great swaths of lands. They were one of the principal landowners under the king, if not comparable to the king. The bishops cast in all their political capital to elevate themselves in the Catholic Church, and they became influential administrators. Everything would be written in Latin, not the Celtic language or the native tongue of that land. It became a consensus and instruction to all bishops that they were to associate all local disasters with sin or sin of the community, which needed to be repented for, and there would need to be offerings of land or some form of physical gift of value. As I stated earlier, these lands that we now call Europe were restricted, and it appears that the Catholic Church wanted everyone to remain illiterate. Based on historical facts, literacy around that time and moving forward through the Dark Ages was very high. The Ecclesia Catholic Church apparently had no intention of changing this as these dark ages dragged on. It will seem to be clear why that would benefit the Collegia Catholic Church so much: There would be many edicts passed and a lot of secular transactions. We call today contract agreements that would be signed over the ages, with the church bishops, monks, and clergy being the only ones with the ability of literacy to read and write. (The Frankish Church. P. 12.)

CHAPTER FIVE

SPIRITUAL BANKRUPTCY

The Ecclesia part of the Catholic Church will start becoming prevalent and pushed to the forefront, from this moment forward. The scale that I referred to in an earlier chapter will become predominant and valuable now because the materialistic aspect of the Catholic Church will start to take shape right here with Clovis the 1st. I think this will be a great example to show the actual network that was in place via Nicene Christianity rebranded Christian philosophy that really powered this network of Ecclesia Enterprise. I will need to reference Gregory of Tours. Gregory was a powerful and very influential historian for the Franks people's history. It would be important to point out point out that Clovis the 1st belong to the original long haired noble race of the royal Franks. (The Frankish Church. P.24)

The Bishop of Remi, Remigius wrote Clovis the 1st after he advanced into Gaul. This letter was to congratulate him on taking control of Belgica Secunda and advised Clovis I on collaborating with the bishops of The Gallo- Roman Church, let's be clear, there was no word in that letter concerning conversion over from his Pagan beliefs and joining the Christian Catholic. But there appeared to be a collaboration that was put together or accepted by Clovis, the first based on the marriage that he had with the Catholic Burgundian Princess Clotilde. She would go on to have two sons, but her wish was to have her sons baptized as Christians. From ancient times we do know that marriages were arranged oftentimes between different family members of royal families as alliances, and this appears to have maybe been one of these situations with the Burgundian Princess. I'm also sure that the princess being Catholic was no coincidence once this collaboration between the bishops appears to take place. Gregory of Tours writes that after the death of his first son, right after the baptism, this kind of drove Clovis the 1st away from the agenda that appears, the Burgundian Princess had in mind, along with the Catholic Bishops, for the King.

Clovis the 1st felt that this had happened because of his denial of his Pagan gods, and this was a major setback for the agenda of the Catholics. But an opportunity would present itself. Once again, when Clovis the 1st went out to face Alamans army and received a major defeat on the battlefield. This defeat made Clovis desperate, and he needed another God, but he needed a war God, and this presented the opportunity for him to receive and consider listening to the bishops as well as his wife with the proposal of a war god, name Christ. Clovis accepted this God on a trial basis and he went out and he won himself a major victory and turn the tables on Alamans Army. Gregory of Tours did not hesitate to point out the similarities between the Milvian Bridge Conversion of Emperor Constantine. Now Clovis the 1st started to listen more to his wife, but she decided to take a step back and enter in the Bishop Remigius of Reims. I would like to take this moment to point out to the readers the consistency that seems to appear every time the conversion of actual king comes about that's needed that helps push forward the agenda of the Ecclesia Catholics. The only thing that I can ask is that you trust when I tell you this will be a consistent pattern you will see throughout this history on the account of The Spiritual Economy. Clovis the 1st had an inner battle. The inner battle that he had was that if he accepted this Nicene Christianity, would his Franks handle the news well? So, he decided to speak to his top warriors or military men about his idea initially, and to his surprise, they accepted. This led to Clovis, the 1st being baptized along with three thousand top warriors at his side. This number is disputed by some academics and maybe even questioned by Gregory of Tours himself. (The Frankish Church.)

After this collaboration with the Catholic Church and the acceptance of the Nicene Christianity by Clovis the 1st. The Franks consisted of nobles and counts this collaboration with the church these men became bishops and abbots long before their followers knew that they had made a change. His aristocratic warriors struggled with baptism being a right that eliminated the need of giving sacrifice and insurance of victory in a battle. With this ancestral past and describing it as a challenge would be an understatement. Yet, the benefit of the alliance with the church was the expansion of the empire to Clovis the 1st appeared to be worth that adjustment. The advantages of conversion by Clovis the 1st was immense. This decision gave him the power now to tap into an extensive network. He gained collaboration in his new expansion of the Empire. Collaboration of the Galileo Roman

Bishops administrated direct control over Gallo Romans who really ran Gaul. The things that this would lead to the support of the church as he invaded the Visigoths, which led to a vast slave trade of over a million people, as stated earlier in the book. With this new network of power through the Ecclesia Church. Land taken, reappropriated, colonization under Ecclesia Catholic Church enterprise and network would be the real reward. (The Frankish Church, page 25.)

Salvian of the 5th century was not a bishop in its traditional sense. Salvian would be somewhat of a free agent at that time, a relic of the past of the old Roman Empire that had failed. Salvian went around preaching nevertheless; other than speaking against the barbarian pagans he seemed to have an infinity for them and looked at them as God's natural children. Salvian being the somewhat apparent corrupt visionary that he was, his desire for the old glory days and what the empire had lost was more potent than his Infinity for the barbarian pagans of that time. Seeing the church as giving the ability to expand the influence of Roman culture to its former glory, Salvian did not only see the church for the promise that it gave to expand Roman culture back to his former glory day was for the parishioners of the church for only the salvation of their souls. To give back to God what was his own, which appeared to be their property and worldly possessions. (The Frankish Church. Pages 2-3.)

I think it's also important to note that the first non-royal charter of foundations of a monastery dates back to 543 AD.(The Frankish Church.) The charter would be a vital instrument for the spreading of the business interests of the church as well as the king.

It is essential that we delve deeper into the aspects of the ecclesia idea as well as this Nicene Christianity and his true purpose, Within my humble opinion. We will have to address the subjects of the monks from what I have exerted, it seemed like the first monks came in with the Frankish church, which would be the Frank monks. (Poitiershistorywalks.com) These monks appear to perceive the Gallic monks. The monks and the monasteries played a considerable role in France and soon to be Europe. The addition to the monks at some point being the nuns did nothing but spread the influence and the power of these banisters. It appears to be more so than the realm of record keeping and the plethora of other things that was imperative and instrumental to the Kingdom and soon to be the actual church.(Wiki) These monks were interested in the aesthetic way of life, but they wanted to have the opportunity to worship in isolation as they seem fit, as well as participate in doing business as I stated earlier in the book. But within my research Hellenism and in specific, Greco Buddhism was the original idea of these monks not exclusive to just the Buddhists because monks are exemplary and other ancient cultures as well. But it appears that the Greco Buddhism really took hold of the Greco or Greek idealism that gave birth to what we now understand as the Roman Republic to the Roman Empire. And soon to be established as the Roman Church. Just as an example. In Egypt, the monks served as well as the priest served as lawyers, judges, officials of government, businessmen, sailors, captains, And even economics, civic law, government statistics, so on and so forth. Even horse breed. (Stolen Legacy, page 172.)

At this point, the church has become the largest landowner. And it appeared as if the bishops had noticed an Achilles heel within the populations, of what will become. These populations were very superstitious even the royal families were highly super-stitious. This made them servants to the church and its bishops that exploited it. Just to give one example of royal families in the hierarchy being affected by these superstitions. Queen Fredegund was convinced that her son's death was based on witchcraft by certain Parisiennes. This superstition was so widely based that it was believed that the witchcraft of men's mistresses would affect their minds. (The Francis Church. Page 41.) King Chilperic was one of those superstitious individuals who was gravely concerned about it. Urged by his Queen, he burns the tax list in a failed attempt to save their son from the plague. After this, the paranoia of superstition led to Maximum giving sprees from the king to the church for the soul, for the salvation of his soul, and his son. Within these royals' minds, the safety of their dynasty. Their legacy was based on the prayers of the church, and no king was willing to take the chance that this may not have been true. This led to massive amounts of money being paid for all types of relics just to find out that they were maybe mice legs, bear claws, and all types of things just to try to ensure that. Evil spirits would be warded off. There became immense profit in the forgery of relics since relics were highly favored and believed in by the superstition of these former barbaric tribesmen or clans. Forgeries of relics should not be a surprise because as we go further, as I think we may have seen in one early instance, there will be many forgeries and even forgeries of actual signed treaties and agreements. But with so much money being made based on the church. This would do nothing but spread more violence, greed, and retributions between individual kings. And of all classes. However, the Frankish kings were highly vulnerable because they felt they had to stay in constant good graces with the church based on God's favor, because they felt their exclusive claim. The rule of the Frankish and Gallo Romans was a direct reflection of this favor. Clovis the 1st, even wrote a letter as proof of that. His association with the church and God and his origin of the long-haired races of the Frankish kings gave him the divine right to rule. (The Frankish Church, pages 41 and 42.)

My perception of this understanding of the superstition of these kings was more deeply rooted. I do believe superstition played a colossal part based on these Klansmen and tribes and their initial religious beliefs, but it appeared in Clovis case that he knew that he would lose control over it. A certain fraction of his empire was without collaboration and the Ecclesia Catholic Bishops' enterprising administrative influencing network over the people. He would lose grip of the people and, with that, A massive part of the newly acquired kingdom. As I stated, these bishops' corporate power cannot be understated. They were extremely powerful, and no secular government or king could rule independently of them. Outside of the reality of the superstitions in these king's minds, it appears that these bishops continue to feed into those fears. As well for leverage, kings knew well enough the spiritual danger they ran into by ignoring these bishop's judgments and the church's councils. It was looked at as heresy if you disobeyed a bishop. (The Frankish Church page 43.) Now, again, I believe that is the underlying factor. But there's no fact that their more potent than this network being put together all up under and in God's name.

We are now in full expression of spiritual bankruptcy. The spirituality that was allegedly in the church, which I suggest, never really existed in the form of the new branding of Christianity. It is exemplary now that this is the case, and whatever spirituality one could have conceived still exists in the church has been bankrupted. The Church has become the most prominent landowner throughout the whole empire. Land or treasury, it didn't matter. There was a monopoly on both, and it would create an inevitable friction spiraling out of control, and secular help was needed. Let me remind you of the definition I placed at the beginning of the book about the feudalistic system. The feudalistic system is a hierarchy, but it provides protection for the lower classes in return. The example that I'm about to put forth is a perfect example of that feudalistic system. And how the secular was able to bring the people in control who were starting to raid, rob, and steal from the actual churches. Here you go, this nasty word again that I referred to earlier. Privilege. Privilege was the actual hallmark of the Ecclesiastical ownership of land, relics, and a monopoly of all wealth it is essential to pay attention to the word ecclesia. Later in the book, I will give you an actual definition of the actual word in the context in which it was created at its conception. I would warn you that there's nothing near what you think and what the definition of the word evolved into. But the actual? The concept of the actual word will help you understand. Why is it where it is? Based on the actual definition of the word and the functions that participated or are exemplified under it, an example of King Chilperic Outburst: "See how my treasury has been drained away and my wealth transferred to the church. Only bishops rule nowadays. My royal honor has deserted me for the bishops in their cities." This is just an example of what the king commented on in outrage, of frustration with what the church and the bishops are doing within his realm. Churches and monasteries all over the Frankish Gaul territories continued attracting all sums and amounts of land, treasure, and all types of endowments from kings, aristocratic, and nobles, all the way down to the layman individual. The use of the wealth that the church accumulated or how or where their store their accumulation of wealth was underprivileged and could not be questioned.

Attacks on church property continue to increase. The motivation didn't appear nefarious; it just seemed people were going where they felt the wealth. Was and robbing it. One example is some robbers that went to a church and stole the church. One was killed, and the others were taken to the King Chilperic. The bishop begged for the one survivor's life. and King Chilperic granted his request for mercy.

King Chilperic sent his son to foreign areas in the western cities to wealthy church properties. And he burned these churches, stoves, sacred vessels, and he slew the clergy, and destroyed monasteries, used nunneries with contempt, and laid waste to all. (The Frankish Church. Pages 45 and 46.) Just based on assumption I wouldn't be surprised if King Chilperic was trying to replace some of all the wealth that was contributed to the bishops within his realm and the treasuries of other churches in other realms. This started to become an organization of raiders versus the ordinary robbers that were characterizing the churches. It seems to me that the church must have gone to the older brother of the Merovingians and asked him to weigh in on the churches being robbed, raided, and so forth. King Guntram delivered an address to his **commanders:**

How are we to win victories when we no longer respect what our fathers respected? They built churches, put all their trust in God, honored the martyrs, venerated the clergy, and won their victories.....Whereas we show no fear of God but devastate his holy places, kill his ministers, disperse and destroy the relics of the saints, and mock them. There cannot be victory while we do such deeds. This is why our hands are powerless, our swords are blunted, and our shields are no longer the defense they once were. If I am to blame for all this, let God's punishment fall on my head. But if it is you who have been disobeying my royal commands, the time is ripe for burying the axe in your heads."

Well, maybe it's me. But after seeing an address like this from the king to his commanders, it appears as if the king feels that perhaps he knows who these raiders are or who they may be. And he had something to tell them about where he would like to park his axe. But one thing was clear: the Merovingian victories depended on not ravaging the churches or robbing. But a return was expected for the king weighing in on the subject. The contributions toward the king started to flow heavily. We could assume that this was somewhat of a tax for calling off his commanders. Within my assumption, it was either pay me or my commanders would take it all. You will see as we continue to go on in this book this sleight of hand. That something would arise between the church. And the different kings regarding wealth, extravagance and the amount of wealth being gained. Mainly by the church, despite the actual king. As we move forward, you also see that there were things that the actual church would do to the king. It's a never-ending cycle of spiritless behavior all toward materialistic expression and greed. There is another crucial fact that I will be remiss not to point out: the donors who gave to the church were not donors who were supposed to provide, and it would just be a one-off. They would have to give to the church or the king consistently. It was never one off. It was consistent, repetitive offerings and gifts that would have to be given; the church would say to these individuals that it was their duty for the sake of their forbearers, souls, and their own. Depending on your family's wealth, this was sort of like insurance or a policy that had to be paid constantly, and you couldn't be late for the security of your soul and your ancestors.

This was a business, and the church was doing very well. In several cases, there was documentation kept by the Nuns of Poitiers to prove that records of donation had been carefully preserved since the foundation of that monastery. It was of grave importance to keep records of all transactions that would take place, and all donations and other things received. There was a trial of Bishop Egidius of Reims, who was accused of disloyalty to Childebert. The bishop claimed that certain estates had been granted to him by royal charter. The bishop even proceeded to show evidence of this actual documentation of this royal charter. There were questions about the authenticity of this document, and after some research, they found out it was a forgery. The individual that was supposed to have granted the **royal charters** were called forth and they assured the court that these signatures and writings were of forgery. The bishop proceeded to demand that he did not forge the documents. However, luck was not on the bishop's side because there was a clerk who kept shorthand copies of all documents. Further papers were found in a room of King Chilperic which was passed into King Childebert's possession after Chilperic's death. (The Frankish Church. Pages. 46- 48.) This stands as an example of the importance that I placed earlier on the monks and the nuns. The clerks who worked in these monasteries were other places of records that they kept up with all transactions. This stands as a testament to that, but not only that, all the families that donated to these monasteries on behalf of churches, kings, and so on kept records in writing of all donations. But this is one of many bishops that were caught with forgeries and several other expressions of documents, as I referred to earlier, as fake relics with all of the profit that the church accumulates from the people. A term was even coined for some of these bishops.

They were classified as aristocratic bishops because of the large sums of wealth they accumulated In God's name. The discovery of forgery was a triumph of justice, a testament to the system's ability to uncover deceit. The 6th-century church had become much more proficient in keeping records of all kinds and at all levels, especially the royal level, but no exception to lower levels. As stated above, family members knew exactly what family members that predated them, as well as current gave to the church as donations. The tradition of giving alms was very important in the minds of the different communities, all for the purpose of when the transition of their souls takes place. Example, Duke Chrodin Stated," That all

these things belong to the church, so that the poor obtain relief.
May win me God's forgiveness." (The Frankish Church, page 48.)

CHAPTER SIX

THE GOD TAX

The Merovingian Empire, at this point, had fully accepted the influence of the church and the numerous Merovingian kings that ruled over vast territory. The Merovingian kings and the church bishops had concluded that neither could rule without the influence of the other. The church bishops have become involved with every aspect of royal life and business. As stated before, these records that were being kept by the monks, the nuns, and all different sorts of legislative groups of bodies were managed by the church based on their ability to read, write, etc. These kings were able to call upon the memory of the church for historical references and collection and memories of past events was always present with these clergy at court. It must be understood that the Merovingian Kings ruled over vast amounts of land, but the land was equally split between the different Merovingian King heir to the throne. However, not all their territories within the kingdoms got along with each other as far as the citizens were concerned. There were criminals and cultural differences between a number of these groups, therefore causing a lot of hatred between each other over relics and different artifacts. These different cities were competitors with each other over so many different things that they ended up building hate for each other and different instances of where the citizens got together and went to war with each other. Bishop Praetextatus had several charges brought against him; one was for bribing the men of Rouen to rebel against their king. (The Frankish Church, page 50.) As the town and the townsmen grew, rebellions broke out all the time, and with people being condemned to death for treason. The actual people would come before judgment was rendered and lynch the individuals themselves. Some of these very large cases made it hard for the actual kings to put these regular rebellions down in quick order. This is why the emphasis of a Bishop was so influential within these cities in keeping control of the population.

The monks and nuns of the 6th and 7th centuries were growing more and more influential, and the creditability for these two groups was impeccable. So, to the point that the guardianship of relics was of paramount importance in this era, and the monks and the nuns were trusted. A value group entrusted with the guardianship of churches and monasteries of these relics that were priceless in their day. Another phenomenon of the day was the growth in the real property market. You had other groups that were outside of kings and clergy, that was starting to become more and more familiar to the prospects of owning large sums of land. A lot of your donors to the church, as well as the different crowns of this day, were starting to become more familiar with this process and started to invest heavily within it. Then there became a question of the inheritance of these properties once property owners passed on, and which they were allowed to pass the properties on to family, but there was no guarantee that the family might not sell it. Then there was always the presence of civil unrest that could cause the loss of property. So, there became a larger and keener interest in monasteries because these monasteries could be left with property, and monasteries were less likely to change hands based on the church's influence within the monasteries. The monastery's prestige oftentimes was based on the forbearer who established it. That gave it certain immunity in some rare cases. This reflects that monasteries were not solely owned, and all power was never given over in most cases to the church; the owners or the establishment of the monasteries did keep some ownership or influence within the monasteries, and this ensured the passing on of inheritance and land via the monastery. There were some cases in which founders looked upon these monasteries as their own, as if it were their property to do what as do with as they please.

One of these examples is Frank Gammo. Gammo established a nunnery on his property of Limours, in which he placed his two daughters, one as an abbess. Later, in a charter dating 697, he remade the house, Saint Germain des Pres. He must have been under the impression that a small nunnery established around that time would need future supervision of a much more influential monastery. But this is an example of someone who felt he could do what he pleased with his nunnery. There will be another example of how inheritance and will structure became much more sophisticated an example was of Bishop Bertram of Le Mans, March, 616. His will was a very complex document, but it gave a clear picture of the mass acquisition of the property. This bishop appeared to enjoy exceptional power within his community. The power that he has within this ecclesiastical nucleus is under the control of the bishop and some bishops of the time. The idea of monasteries would fit perfectly in this pattern of immense influence. As stated before, the church was a very large landowner. And there are many dioceses in the 7th century. Bishop Bertram had made many, numerous purchases of property in urban and rural within his diocese, and he paid close and sharp attention to the details between his Episcopal church monasteries and his relationships. Based on it, it is subject to Episcopal control, which also indirectly gave the bishop a lot of influence over it. There were some exceptional monasteries that seem to have immunity from any influence of an ecclesiastic or kings. One monastery was St Calias, which enjoyed immunity for generations. Exactly why it received this level of immunity no one knows. What is known is that the foundation of the house was on land gifted by King Childebert. Through Gregory of Tours, we know that in 576, King Chilperic used St. Calais as a prison for his rebellious son Merovech. (The Frankish Church, pages 61 and 62.) I want the reader to make a note for future reference in this book of the use of monastery and Ecclesiastical Church properties for imprisonment, not only for royal family members. However, for the average everyday citizen, outside of those found guilty in the ecclesial Church, monasteries and church facilities were also used. The king would be charged rent to imprison people for violations against the state. Now, we will be introduced to a bishop familiar with Asceticism and this gentleman's name was Bishop Columbanus. Columbanus was acquainted with this Asceticism from the Irish church via Cassian. Columbanus required strict discipline from his monks as well as he practiced in his life. This monastic lifestyle was an older of the Eastern Church called coenobitism.

Columbanus was also credited with introducing private penance to the continent. What is clear is that this formed a major moral teaching direction for his monks. Confession and absolution are not confined to just a single action as with Canonical Penance. The bishop believed that an individual should be in a constant state of confession. Columbanus own monastery requires confession before eating as well as bedtime. He facilitated an intimate relationship, priestly relationship between confession and dependence of the individuals in his monastery and the neighborhood of his monastery. He did receive some pushback from the Frankish

Church bishops. They have become too except his teaching, and it basically kept his society burden in a constant state of remorse for possible sins committed and these communities needed constant reassurance. Under Bishop Columbanus, confessions became a constant state of daily life. Private opinions became a regular practice acknowledged by the Council of Chalon Of circa 650 private penance was officially recognized.' we judge it to be of use to all'. The bishops that followed Columbanus' teachings owe, a great debt to the bishop. However. This appreciation in his life was not experienced to the degree that he was appreciated much later at the Council of Chalon in 603 when he appeared to be subject to possible exile from the church. He was forced to defend his position. But what stands out to me is that so early in the 6th century, he made a reference to race: 'For we are all joint members of one body, whether Franks or British or Irish or whatever our race may be.' Gaul can contain everyone.'(65- 66 The Frankish Church)

Within the Frankish church, Columbanus remain a foreigner within their minds, but one thing was clear, Columbanus cared and rebuke sin where he found it and his concern was with the salvation of his followers. And it also appears that the bishop was not afraid to challenge the lifestyle of the of kings when it came to morals. During Columbanus's lifetime, it was challenged by the Frankish Church at every turn. I find it to be extremely interesting the consumption of his views by that same community within the Frankish Church. After his transition from this life. It appeared to be a new philosophy that had been adopted, called the mixed rule. This mix rule consisted of Saint Benedict's and Bishop Columbanus religious lifestyle philosophies. The legislation of Columbanus was moral and penal in flavor. Admirable as a guide to ascetics. In comparison, that of Benedict was a way of life beautifully orchestrated to the needs of a community. They blended well, though in the end, it would be the contribution of Columbanus that would atrophy. (The Frankish Church. Page 70.)

St. Eligius was the distinguished man of humble birth? Their fortunes came through his ability as a goldsmith, which put him in a very high society. And it brought him to the Royal Court as a goldsmith. Through his ability, he received the foundation charter of his monastery at Solignac. This charter placed the family under royal protection and exempt from any Episcopal influence. This was a royal gift in the form of a charter that freed it from any ecclesial influence or control. Eligius, well then, in my opinion, made one of the best business decisions that could be made at that time.

He recruited some of the monks within the area, but the estate he received came with slaves. (Slavery, again, is a part of everyday societal life in the 6th century as well. King Clovis II wife Balthild, was once an enslaved Anglo-Saxon) and he freed them who came with the estate to become monks. (Eligius was named Bishop of Noyon, continued his ecclesial life, and founded a nunnery in Paris. Eligius was one of the many who was under the influence of Columbanus. Who became monastic founders representing one of many that adopted the Columbanus lifestyle but express in the mixed rule. There was a group of servants to royal families that became the benefactors of lands. Under the protection of the royal families and not under the influence of the ecclesial churches. Which ended up dedicating their lands to monasteries and nunneries but under the mixed rule. But just from my observation, two separate kings under the Merovingian supported this mixed rule lifestyle. They had it under its protection so as not to be influenced by the Frankish Church.

These charters were given to these families that continued to grow and found monasteries. It appeared to me, just from the reading I was doing, as if it was some−controlled Experiment: A mixture of two different philosophies of Columbanus and Saint Benedict to be placed in one community to observe how it would thrive outside the established Episcopal churches. (The Frankish Church, pages 70 - 71.) This mixed rule would be very successful, and it would be widely successful in the actual church. But the private penance theory it would be one that would give birth to a constant state of what appeared to me to be sin/ debt. As we proceed with the book, you will see that it will be very profitable for the church. Philosophy was written by two honorable men, namely Bishop Columbanus and Saint Benedict. Teaching a deeper spiritual-based understanding of salvation appears to be what would become twisted into commercial subjugation of communities of non-enslaved poor but free people who would become subjects on their land under a feudalistic scheme unescapable by any branch of humanity and will be called commerce.

CHAPTER SEVEN

HEAVENS DEBIT & EARTH'S CREDIT

F or the sake of not extending this book longer than necessary. In my attempt to keep the book a short read, it was impacted with in-depth information so that the reader could continue to follow up on research in their own time. This chapter will be loose but consistent with the patterns of information that are or have been enlisted in the book thus far. I want to warn the reader that this chapter will begin to itemize along a timeline to move the process along quicker while arriving at the points that I choose to reflect on to help the reader see the overall vision. But after this chapter, I will go along a strict timeline stating different world events within the church that will lead in the direction of our current state in the world.

This chapter is about to set into motion what is about to come. We are about to enter the 7th century, and the world is rapidly changing. The foundation is in the 7th century, which is the mid-point of what will reflect the future of what would become Europe based on the structure that the Catholic Church is putting into place via treaties and our current date understanding of contracted agreements. That's weighing heavily on the history of its ancestors, the Greeks and the Romans Hellenistic gumbo. Everything stated in this book as of now will be built upon in the 7th century moving forward, but it will be turned into a global God-based tax system imposed on the world by the Catholic Church. This leads to a debit and credit system based on today's understanding but using spiritual guidelines that are reflected in a secular world, and the church will begin to underwrite sin by selling God's forgiveness for a privileged few that could afford it and the rest would be damned to hereditary servitude under the description of slavery. Let me now do a small review, but a tailored understanding of these terms I'm about to define as we move forward will help the reader. Discerning precisely what I'm attempting to show from a historical standpoint. The Catholic Church, in my opinion, should be renamed under the definition that I believe it accurately fits, which is the **Ecclesia Church**. Both terms, as in ecclesia and church, found their foundation within the Greek civilization. What I will do for you here is show you the history of these two terms as they translate into today's english as I proceed with the history of the Catholic Church, you will have a much better understanding of why my conclusion is as such.

The word **Church** derives from the Scottish word Kirk or, should I say, Kirke. Now, the word Kirk, and we will drop the E just for simplicity. It derives from the Greek word Circe. There was a Greek goddess by the name of Circe. This goddess was known for seducing people back into her home with drunkenness and all other types of promiscuous and questionable behavior. Once you were in the goddess' home she would close the door and feed off the people she seduced into her home. I guess that can be interpreted as literal, or it can be interpreted as figuratively were living off the people financially.

Now as for the word **Ecclesia:** *Ecclesia was derived from the Greeks. And signify the legislative body that governed ancient Athens long before Christianity was invented. The first essential act of the Ecclesiastes was to suppress Gnosticism and confiscate its vast accumulation of wisdom and knowledge in order to control the education of future generations in a manner that adjusts mankind to its purposes. Therefore, Gnostic wisdom was not wholly lost to the world, but its great universal educational system It was supplanted. It is a well-established historical fact, not denied by the Church, that it required about 500 years to accomplish this immersion of Gnosticism and to degrade the new generations in ignorance equal to the state of imbecility. History again points its accusing finger at the living evidence. The horrible results of such a crime against nature and mankind are pictured in the Dark Ages.... Not even Priests or prelates were permitted to learn to read or write. Even bishops could barely spell out their Latin during this period of mental darkness and ignorance. The masses were trained in intolerance. Bigotry, fanaticism, and superstitious fears of an invisible power secretly controlled by the Church, all of which began a state of hysteria and imbecility. Through this terrorism, popes seized control of the temporal power. Retaining this control for nearly 500 years, they appointed. And disposed of Kings at will? Hence, they dictated legislation to their end and proposed the very essence of government. This process of legislating evil into mankind is to vindicate rights. That damned the doctrine of original sin, which slanders nature and insults all mankind. Initially, the motive* *was to confiscate the intellects of man, but modern policies are much more concerned with confiscating your personal rights and property. (Christianity before Christ. Page 122. John G Jackson.)*

I firmly believe, and I think I have indicated why I believe that the Ecclesia Church, under the definition described above, is a version of the Catholic Church before the Common Era. As I proceed, it will become much more apparent. An indisputable historical account is reflected in its behavior.

Privilege, indeed, was the hallmark of ecclesiastical ownership, whether of land, treasure, or relics. King's grasping the significance of unceasing donations to churches. **King Chilperic:' See how my treasure has been drained away and my wealth transferred to the church! On the bishops rule now a day! My royal honor has deserted me for the bishops in their cities!** *(The Frankish Church, page 45.)*

The Christian emperor of Rome, Constantine, six years after passing the Edict of Tolerance of 313 AD in Milan on behalf of Christians. He ruled that if an owner whipped his white slave to death." He should not stand in any criminal accusation if the slave dies, and all statutes of limitations and legal interpretations are hereby set aside." (They were white, and they were slaves. Page 7. Michael A Hoffman II)

*The Romans enslaved thousands of early white inhabitants of Great Britain who were known as" Angles". From which we derive the term" Anglo-Saxon". As a description of the English (***Angle- Land: Eng-land***) race. (They were white, and they were slaves. Page 7.)*

The Catholic Church was very much a part of all these activities stated above. And as I continue throughout the book, you will see that he was even in the furtherance of it. But all these activities were practiced pretty much so in the Greek culture that predated the Roman Culture. Both of these cultures were slave societies that had a vested interest in colonizing each other for the purpose of feeding the demands of this market and enriching the governments that would later on become influenced by the culture that eliminated the majority of the fighting between what Bishop Columbanus referred to in circa 603 A.D. in The Council of Chalon where he was called to explain himself when he referred to The holy man within the conference as Being of different races. (The Frankish Church)

But allow me to introduce you to another term: Peters Pence. Peters Pence was an ecclesiastical tax placed on sovereign kings of countries. We will come to know this term as **tithing** or a **tithe.** The common folk will come to know it as a 10th of one's income property concerning wealth paid to the church.

The seed plot of this tradition may have been a letter from **Pope Leo III***, written in 797 or 798, to Cenulf, Offa's successor, asking for continuance of the 365 Mancuses which Offa had promised in a synod attended by papal legates to give annually in perpetuity to Saint Peter for alms of the poor and for the lights of the Church. The synod was held at Chelsea in 787. (Financial Relationships of the Papacy with England to1327. Page 8.)*

Pope Gregory *Received 300 mancuses in 857 after Ethelwulf's visit to Rome in 855. This was done after his return during the two remaining years of his life, as recorded by Asser in his will. He ordered 300 mancuses. To be sent yearly to Rome. 100 Was to be used for the lights of the Church of Saint Peter, 100 for the lights of the Church of St. Paul, and 100 for the Pope. Ethelwulf annually grants a penny to St. Peter from every house in his Kingdom in turn for the papal privilege regarding penance. In addition, 300 mancuses are to be sent to Rome annually. (Financial relationships of the papacy with England to 1327.)*

This century will be plagued by forgeries. An effort to gain more property at whatever Or whomever the expense. The Abbotts that had control of the abbeys were starting to use these properties for prisons and other purposes, charging the state or, in some cases, the different ecclesial individuals for rent for the use of these properties as such. The Merovingian dynasty is starting to slip, and with that, the Frankish church to the Carolinian up-and-coming military superiority. An example of this is in 688. The Austrasia magnate Pepin II won control of Neustria and thus of Paris at the battle of Tertry near St. Quentin. (The Frankish Church. Page 131). These were starting to become turbulent times, and one thing was clear: donations to the church had to be consistent and continue to flow. Anything that was to be secured would be secured through payment, including loyalty.

As the church became more and more secular, where profit became the main objective, and this was all-inclusive with the property of people or actual traditional estate property like in the case of monasteries and abbeys. Monasteries and abbeys became the main places for prisons, and these prisons were not just for political opponents or royal disgruntled family members now. In some cases, these monasteries and advisees were required to have prison cells inside of them for criminals or offenders of the ecclesiastical canon. As I stated before, rents were necessary for these individuals, so it became another source of making and gaining profit as prison became more and more popular; there was not a stretch or shortage of space for these violators of the law, ecclesiastical or secular. There have been many cases where prisoners have been changed, deprived of food, and actual corporal punishment, which included forms of ritual humiliation. What I found to be very interesting was that it seemed like all the religious or ecclesiastical institutions were the primary sources of prison space for violators of secular law, as well as the ecclesiastical form. These are a few of the examples of the prisons of religious or spiritual institutions that became more and more secular in the pursuit of profit: Monastic prisons, Inquisitorial prisons, and Diocesan prisons. (Ecclesiastical prisons. Wikipedia.)

As the Catholic Church became more secular, it started to look for temporal powers. Agreements and treaties between the Church and sovereigns were starting to dissipate. The lands were under threat by the Moors of Northern Africa, and they were advancing. As stated throughout the book, over many centuries, the church had accumulated massive amounts of land, riches, and much treasure. The different tribes of what would become Europe were turning back to their true nature of war disagreement and constantly looking to colonize each other and their neighbors for or in search of property and treasure. The church would find itself being preyed upon. As well. But it appeared that these kings had learned a thing or two from having the ecclesiastical bishops at court and seeing how the church often used forged documents to claim—properties as belonging to them, allegedly from being donated from the Emperor Constantine.

Now, the rule of the day appeared to be that charters were being produced and brought before kings to try to solve property disputes. Which would be seen as we proceed, that the word charter would be the father of our current day corporation. Charles Martel was in power now and had stopped the Arab advance. Charles Martel had no issue with commandeering the property of the churches. He took several abbey estates and handed them to supporters. He also appeared to look the other way when some of his supporters decided to seize several of the estates for themselves. But there appeared to be a new introduction to the way of doing business. For example, *there was a very high value placed on the written contracts, as illustrated by the case of St. Denis reclaiming an oratory in Hainault from a certain Hormungus rector of Marseille, who produced in justification the first known authentic forged diploma. St. Denis also won back property from the abbess of Septmeules, who seemed equally to have tried her hand at forgery. It was not easy, even for Charles Martel, to prevent others from nibbling at the scattered properties of so rich a house. (The Frankish Church. Page 133.)*

Archbishop Egbert's copy of the letter of St. Boniface and others to King Aethelbald of Mercia. Charles had recently died after a long and painful illness because of his seizure of church property.

Archbishop Hincmar of the ninth century: Charles had to burn in hell for the sins of a whole generation. (The Frankish Church. Page 134)

Some historians state that the effect of Charles Martel's seizure of church property cannot be adequately or accurately disclosed. *The taking of church lands, whether outright or on a temporary basis, whether with some legal color or without it, goes back in time and far behind Charles Martel. The wealthier churches became, the likelier it was to happen. There were several possible reasons for this. Plain robbery was one, and the pages of Gregory of Tours provide many early instances. (The Frankish Church, page 134.)*

It appears that the things for the Catholic Church started to repeat themselves. Where the church enjoyed some centuries under the Merovingian Dynasty, a stable representation of the church and the secular side. There appeared to be a retrograde back to the earlier area before them where bishops and areas were becoming more influential, as they were at one point, and those communities were starting to depend on these bishops, and then you had warrior bishops that were starting to invade areas and take the land as they were before. The secular description of Dukes and Counts and several other titles did not ring with the people anymore. The Carolinians, who will meet very soon, were also accused of several secular efforts toward the church property, but nothing could compare based on some historical accounts of the abuse by the bishops. These bishops were so influential in certain areas that they became a dynasty of bishops. Things had grown so bad too, to the point that municipal authorities would have to take on ecclesiastical titles in order to maintain any sense of power among the power communities. One such example of these powerful bishops was *Bishop of Auxerre Savaric; by force of arms, he took control of Orleans, Nevers, Tonnerre, Avallon, and Troyes. Finally meeting his end once he marched on Lyon. (The Frankish Church.)*

This was clearly a new game that had not been observed for hundreds of years. Charles Martel, as the leader of the Franks, was a true reflection of that time after putting a stop to the advance of the Arabs. He was joined by one of these very powerful bishops named Bishop Ainmar, who appeared to have been of good use to Martel. History tells us that once things settled squarely under the King's control, *He turned without hesitation upon Ainmar and got rid of him. The property of the Holy See now shanks to a hundred manses, we are told. The bishop was deprived of control over his monasteries. Charles was doing two things: he was availing himself of the ecclesiastical property to reward his loyal followers, and he was removing a bishop too closely identified with the interest of the local Aristocracy. (The Frankish Church.)*

Just from the points expressed above, it is clear that these are different and trying times facing the church at this point. Judging manic people, along with the number of the other clans, were looked at as Barbarians and pagans. That idea was becoming formed, and even though some were Christians, Christians were labeled under a different description of the Catholic Church. Nevertheless, the policy at the time appeared to have changed, and all Christians were looked at as Christians and needed to be under one spiritual and theoretic roof. Missionaries were a major source of creating this atmospheric, social-communal change. The Merovingian prince's military power was the cornerstone of the stability and spread of this brand of Christianity stating this "lets us make no mistake because, without them, it would not have been possible". These missionaries who went off into foreign lands were the result of a powerful military and oftentimes ended up being forward military bases in the event that this new brand of Christianity was resisted. By stating this, it can only be expected that the demand for pagans at this time was at an ultimate high. The willingness of these missionaries to be right there to save you was never in short supply.

Never be the one short on proof and be willing to express that. I don't want the reader to feel that I was stating that the form of Christianity being spread at the time was a new brand of Christianity. It may come as a surprise that there was a need for missionaries, especially from specific areas like the Anglo-Saxon Clerics. *A Benedictine monk and a former pupil of St. Wilfrid. He knew something of the resources of the papacy. He arrived in Frisia in 690 and turned at once to Rome for permission to preach. The Pope was the man to license missionary work, as every Anglo-Saxon cleric knew, moreover. Willibrord wanted Roman relics for the churches he hoped would replace Pagan shrines. (The Frankish Church. Page 145)*

Sure. Just from a legal standpoint, and clearly, this version of Christianity couldn't belong to God because you need a license to practice or preach it. But as we go along, you will soon see that this is just the beginning of many things that you would need to license.

Clearly, there was a change on the horizon, and nothing could subvert this change that was coming, and it was coming rapidly. The winds of change and the power structure were evident or becoming evident. While the Catholic Church was looked upon as the savior of the people, it had reached a point where it required a savior. The Carolinian dynasty was about to begin, but it started with a question of the **Potens' persona**. Pippin of the Carolinians, sent to emissaries to Rome in 751, was an Anglo-Saxon man, and the other was a Frank. They were instructed to ask the Pope this question: ***Should a ruler enjoy no power rightly continue to bear the title of king? How could one be a king without Potestas?***

In a word, the Pope had been invited by two churchmen of very different backgrounds to pronounce the Merovingians and anachronism. (The Frankish Church. Page 166)

I don't believe it is known to history. The pope's exact response, but one thing is clear: The pope obliged the Carolinians and fulfilled their request. Bringing an end to the Merovingians Dynasty in 751. Pippin and his wife were crowned King & Queen of the Franks. Making an official ending to the long-haired Merovingian's reign. King Childeric and his heir were taken to St. Bertin Monastery, which for them was equivalent to a modern-day form of house arrest in a luxurious palace but at St Bertin. Childeric's family has faithfully served the papacy and its interests for hundreds of years. In the end, the reward they received was to be taken off into humiliation and live in the monastery. Comfortably for the rest of their lives in shame. The church no longer had a use for them.

Pope Gregory VII, *looking back on the part played by his distant predecessor Zacharias. He commented that the last Merovingian was not disposed of for moral defects but because he was not useful. A king must be suitably gifted. He must have utilitas. (The Frankish Church. Page 166)*

Pippin III: Now the new Emperor of the Franks. Needing to establish himself in power and to enrich his supporters. Amongst his warriors set on an expedition to the north of Italy to bring back plenty of booty for his coffers as well as to reward his warriors within his ranks. Which was one surefire way to keep them out of the local churches and other places of wealth, doing what they did best rob. Yet there was another problem that the pope had foresight enough to see, and this problem was an old problem that dated back to the 3rd or 4th century. And this was the Lombards. The Lombards had always had ambitions to rule all of Italy, back from the days of the 3rd and 4th centuries when they were accredited, with the first version of the promissory note being a very well-established merchant family. The Catholic Church and it is established land were under threat by the Lombards. This threat was an imminent threat that looked like it was to place a hold on the property of the church. And maybe even in the church as we know it and that is reflected in this statement Quote:

By 750, the papacy could legitimately feel that Rome was threatened by the Lombards, as were the remaining outposts of imperial power in Italy. Only the Franks could save Rome. Such was the conclusion of Pope Stephen II. Who succeeded Zacharias in 752. A secret mission was dispatched to Peppin. To emphasize the menace that Rome faced and to beg for an interview with him. (The Frankish Church. Page 167)

Words cannot express the importance of this historical event. On the one hand, you had the Moors that moved into Europe and ruled part of it, if it were not for Charles Martel stopping their advance, they could have run through the entirety of Europe. The Moors of North Africa ruled parts of Europe for Circa 711 years. Which in turn calls the Catholic Church and its position in Italy into question. This explains the chaotic moments that basically repeated the past of what the Catholic Church had got under control in the lands that would become Europe. However, it is crucial that the reader pay attention to the negotiations and the contracts through treaties being made, as well as the forgeries. That you would now witness again at its very highest level. I would also like to reiterate that this time was during the Dark Ages, when the majority of Europe, according to several historians, expressed that the illiteracy rates were very high. I would be remiss not to point out that it was well documented that even your royal families. Kings could not read and we know from the ecclesia doctrine, as well as the soon-to-be Catholic Church reading, was something that they did not want to promote. And we could see, and we will see, why this was important to implement. The rest of what I'm about to reveal to you will set the tone for the remaining 1000 years and how business will be executed. In my opinion, this will be the groundwork for what will create our current economic system. As we proceed in this book, you will see what I'm talking about as the church creates two sides. One could be the spiritual side, and one could be the side of the physical body that would later turn private and public. Historically, before this point, the Church dealt predominantly with the spiritual side and let the kings deal with the secular side. Now, you will see that the Church will start to enter the temporal part which is secular. This reflects what I stated early in the book, which was the actual goal of the Catholic Church and why I called it the Ecclesia Church. Pope Stephen II and after began an audience with Pippin III. The king would send troops to bring the Pope to him through the land of the Lombards. In my opinion to ensure the pope made it to him safely. Pippin would send his son out to bring the Pope in Charlemagne the Great at the very young age of 12 Years old. Before I express this example, it is also important to state exactly what happened in this historical event. The Papal State was not a state prior to this moment in history, and the events that would take place will be the beginnings of our understanding of the Papal State:

The Charlemagne made his debut in a company with a Pope. The process entered Panthion on 6 January 754, Pippin holding the pope's bridle. Negotiations follow. Pippin, as a result, undertook to oust the Lombards from the exarchate Ravenna and restore the territories and rights of the Roman Republic to the pope, though, in fact, they belonged to the emperor. All these were now represented as the rights of St. Peter. It may well be that at this stage the pope exhibited for inspection a Roman forgery in which there may well be elements of truth known as the Donation of Constantine, according to this, along with much else. Constantine had endowed Pope Silvester I and his successors with Rome, Italy, and the West. The forgery bears all the marks of a literary composition by some member of the Lateran staff who knew how to make intelligent use of a much older composition, The so-called Act of Silvester. Plainly, it is an early step, perhaps the first, toward the birth of the paper state as the future was to Know it. (The Frankish Church. Page 168)

After some discussion between the Lombards and Pippin, it appeared that the Lombards were reluctant to adhere to the meeting of mines of giving up territory that was donated through Constantine's donation to St. Peters; Pippin led forces against the Lombards. There were several years before Rome was safe from the threat of the Lombards. I believe it was in the year 759. This marks the moment in history when the Church became spiritual and secular. They had obtained the goal of having spiritual as well as temporal power. I have not seen any clear indication of this, but I would like to suggest that you really haven't heard anything about the Frankish Church being under the rule of the Frank king anymore. It appears as if the negotiation between Pippin and the pope were, the pope gave up a number of concessions to Pippin of the Carolinians, he also received several very high titles and the Church's support for his lineage being on the throne through the threat of excommunication of anyone that would attempt to overthrow them. The Pope appeared to have taken over the authority of the Frankish Church and consumed it inside the Catholic Church.

The sole purpose of this book is to make it a quick read. The following chapter 8 will be, as I stated earlier, a timeline. This will be a timeline that I guide you through, covering almost 1000 years of very important events that will lead to my understanding of how we arrive in our current form of society and how it was influenced by the history we have already covered. I may make some brief statements on some of the articles I placed inside chapter 8 to give you a breast of the depth of the documents or the historical events and their effect on the history or events that will follow within that timeline. The purpose of my conclusion. Chapter 8, in that style, is only to allow the reader to come to their own conclusion and not just see or identify with the things I have stated based on the history and my observation of it. I can only hope that the reader continues to research for themselves. This is nothing more than just a pointer pointing you to specific places to help you further your study and understanding the grasp of Western structure and government, which, in my opinion, was born out of the spiritual or religious contractual treaty agreements that would become the template of what we would come to understand reflected in the secular under the description of THE STATE.

CHAPTER EIGHT

THE GOD-BASED ECONOMY AND A TIMELINE OF EVENTS

N ow we have arrived at the moment of truth, a truth that you will or won't see based on your God-given ability to KNOW........and KNOW because that little voice inside of you that always seems to KNOW......... and KNOWS I have told you. Good luck, and here we go.

With the Persian Empire came the Aramaic language. The Aramaic language, the metaphor of sin as burden, was replaced with the commercial metaphor of sin as a debt that demanded repayment. The idea of sin as debt suffused the Jewish world of the Second Temple Period. (Christianscholars.com. February the 14th, 2022.)

The Pope of Rome in the Middle Ages would stand above kings. Ruled by the Church. The Papal State property always has been focused on kings in which the ecclesia church won, and the kings would directly and indirectly rob the church. The Ecclesia Church would now have no rivals. Property was the sole purpose which gave way to defining property rights and by whom the privilege to own would be granted along with the titles and change of title. Which caused the creation of property law. What may come as a surprise, but a gross example is that marriage was also a part of those property rights that belong to this privileged group of men. (30,000 Names before Jehovah, page 65. The Frankish Church, page 171.)

Bishop Columbanus: Private penance becomes a factory line of gifts and offerings, bringing confessors under a would become extensive property grabbing Ponzi scheme of self-identified centers of the commercialized version of sin but now directly associated with debt. That also drained and taxed everything from the Freeman as Alms for salvation of your soul on the spiritual side and a creation of laws on the secular side to duplicate that same draining and taxing, but by new creation by the color of law that would be described as THE STATE (STATE: created based on the definition of the word STATUS; in terms of jurisdiction or authority given by created SECULAR/ TEMPORAL [WORLDLY or of THE WORLD – NON SPIRITUAL JURISDICTION] LAWS.). At one point or another you would become property for insolvency (sin/debt) that would call into question your in-alienable rights granted to you by God. The Bible would be brought in and all the rebranded scriptures would be introduced against you in the Ecclesia Court of Spiritual/Non-secular jurisdiction [Left side of the balance sheet representing DEBITS/ ASSETS], which would soon be patterned after by the king, which represented the physical/ secular (WORLDLY) side of jurisdiction [right side of the balance sheet representing CREDITS/ LIABILITIES] which he would give That power under the title of Monarch that would become again the bases of the creation of the state as another body or vassal: THE STATE.

Allowing an in-alienable to be stripped away from you or the spiritual part of you, taking your inheritance given to you by God and protected on the private side. Which is on the left side of the balance sheet. Allowing your insolvent debt to pull you on the secular/worldly physical side of sin unpaid debt column of the accounting ledger, making you alienable (separated from the spiritual inalienable you, making you alienable physical/secular). Charges are brought, and once convicted of or found guilty, you are now labeled an alien with no rights, stripped of any right given by God (spiritual/non-secular left side of the balance sheet with debits/ assets). Then someone comes along and pays your debt: re-mission, then places a-lien on your body, and you become a slave and put into slavery. The gift of rebranded. Nicaean Christianity. Stay close as I guide you through this thousand-year history; this is all open to your interpretation.

CHAPTER NINE

GOD'S LAW ENSLAVED THE WORLD

I would like to start this chapter by reminding you about the initial beginnings of this work. The part where we start to speak about Emperor Constantine in the 3rd century. The basis of all that we are about to discuss hinges on what we will come to learn as the Donation of Constantine. The rights claimed by the Roman Catholic Church will be based on documentation that some throughout history have called forgeries based on whatever the Pope was trying to accomplish at the time I will hinge upon it. I will conclude at the end of this timeline by giving my theory of why this so-called Donation of Constantine was so relevant based on additional historical facts. Allow me to input a passage from the Black's Law Dictionary that gives the definition of the **Roman Catholic Church:**

The juristic personality of the Roman Catholic Church, with the right to sue and to take and hold property, has been recognized by all systems of European law since the 4th century. It was formally recognized between Spain and the Papacy and by Spanish laws from the beginning of the settlements in the Indies. Also, our treaty with the Spanish in 1898, whereby its property rights were solemnly safeguarded. Municipality of Ponce versus Roman Catholic Church. (Black Law Dictionary, 6th edition, 1891- 1991.)

This year reflects the initial agreements, as I stated earlier and throughout the entire book, that Europe is a reflection of treaties and contract agreements between tribes, or should I say clans of European tribes, from the very earliest of ages with the Roman Catholic Church, which would at some point become headed by the Papacy. Throughout history, it has been accepted in the forms of law adopted by this ecclesia institution. And this power grew from its conception of non-secular to the realm of secular.

At the beginning of this timeline, I must introduce several phrases and individuals that will frame or shape the next thousand years. Millennia. As I proceed through this final chapter, you will be surprised and maybe overwhelmed mentally. With some patterns I introduced, you can track them on your own basis and dig further into them. In conclusion, I will tie or bring many of these ends together that may show an example of what I perceive to be patterns that lead to this truth that I'm trying to share with you inside this work. Let me introduce a small teaser to you by stating my opinion that the Roman existence or expression of democracy and government was nothing but a reflection of what the Greeks had done prior. Still, they completed their objective or the objective of the Greeks in this expression, which leads me to give you the philosopher that will coin many of the ideals. That would end up being debated within these millennia and become law. Using his logic Aristotle is this Greek philosopher's name.

Sentences of circa 1150: This new doctrine was largely the work of two generations of Theologians teaching in the cathedral schools of Paris in the early decades of the 12th century. Their collective efforts were written up by Peter Lombard in his Sentences of circa 1150. Purgatory was brilliantly logical, if not the only possible reconciliation of several. Separate disjointed passages of the Old and New Testament, powered by the application of newly discovered principles of **Aristotelian** *logic, Come. Which* **has** *been lost to the West since the 5th century, when firsthand knowledge of many Greek classics had faded away with the unraveling.* **(Time Magazine: A Brief History of Purgatory)**

These two theologians, whom I will describe now, were critical. They coined or shaped the future of this 12th-century period that the passage above is speaking about, using or leaning heavily on Aristotelian logic.

Thomas Aquinas: circa 1225-Seven, March 1274. *Dominican Friar, priest, influential philosopher and theologian, and a jurist of the tradition. Scholasticism.* (Wikipedia)

Henry of Segusio, usually called Hostiensis (C. 1200-6 or 7 November 1271), *Was an Italian canonist of the thirteenth century, born at Susa (Segusio) in the ancient Diocese of Turin. Italian Canonist. Papal Plenitudo Potestatis.* (Wikipedia)

Allow me to give you a small example of Henry of Segusio, or should I say Hostiensis, Aristotelian logic of the fifth century that was reintroduced into the minds of the Roman Empire. That was the beginning of the neo-Ecclesia Greek philosophy:

For Hostiensis the law, as well as all political authority, were derived from God. Because of this, all princes exercise authority by divine mandate. Civil law was divine. Because the emperors who created that law were placed in authority by God. Despite this, however, civil law was inferior to Canon law.

The reason for this is that the pope's authority was even closer to the divine than that of a secular princess. Because the pope was the vicar of God, he acted on God's authority, from which he, the pope, derived his own authority. Thus, whoever the pope acted deiure, he acted as God. Therefore, Canon law, since it was created by the pope, was established by God. This is because Canon law was based on the Bible, and God had given his vicar, the pope, the authority to interpret—that text. Thus, Canon law was divine not because it came directly from God but because of the end it sought (The spiritual well-being of Christians) And because of the dignity of the Pope, from which the Canon law emanated.

Hostiensis believed that the pope should follow positive law he was not bound by it. The pope could not be tried for any crime except that of heresy, in which case the pope could be subject to The Ecclesia. For any other violation of law, the pope could be judged by no one save God. According to him, the pope was imbued with the authority of the two swords, interpreted as spiritual and temporal power.

The spiritual was superior to the temporal in the following three aspects. In dignity, for the spirit is greater and more honorable than the body, in time, for it was earlier, and in power for it not only institutes the temporal power, but also with the authority to judge it, while any man could not judge the Pope except cases of heresy. The Pope entrusted temporal authority to the emperors but retained the right to reclaim that authority in virtue of the PLENITUDO POTESTATIS, which he possesses as the vicar of Christ. Indeed, the temporal power of the pope was so complete. Hostiensis consider it a mortal sin for a temporal ruler to disobey the Pope in temporal matters. This view of papal authority in temporal matters also applied to the kingdoms of non-Christians. Because to him, all sovereignty had been taken away from non-Christians and transferred to the faithful. When Christ came into the world, this translation of power was first made to the person of Christ, who combined the function of priesthood and kingship, and this sacerdotal and kingly power was transferred to the Pope. (Wikipedia. Henry of Segusio.)

It's important to pay very close attention to what you just read and understand as much as the legal documents of that day. Setting precedents for what authorities the pope or the office of the papacy would have. As it describes, Canon law was more powerful than the actual temporal or secular law of the world. Clearly defining the left and the right columns of the accounting sheet that I'm trying to suggest. I showed you just a touch of some of this theologian philosophy of the Aristotelian logic to set the table for what I will start introducing to you that may be not reassuring to some. According to these documents, what would become Canon law, as stated above and found in the Black's Law Dictionary, will be introduced into actual time, secular law must be honored that the power of the pope was not ruling as appointed by God, but the understanding of the Vicar of Christ. He was God himself on earth. Therefore, from this point forward if the term ruling by divine right is stated, you would know that that divine right is not what would come to one's mind as God because according to this theory of theologian philosophy, God on earth is the pope, so ruling by divine right would be by the authorization of the pope, given the authority given to him on the spiritual end—the left side to transfer to the right side of the secular world.

12th century would look back to their founding ideologies but with absolute spiritual and secular **AUCTORITAS ECCLESIE.** There would be no need to disguise its intentions now. Greek ecclesia practices and examples of governance would be the goal via the views of. Aristotelian philosophy of debate would create ground-work to create a legal system with the goal of manifesting a neo-Ecclesia C.E version of its B.C.E Ecclesia predecessor.

I know I have stated it throughout the book about the Ecclesia. I gave numerous examples and different definitions for this group's influence back in Athens and other Greek city-states at that time. For the sake of not having to thumb all the way back to different parts of the book, let me update your memory here concerning the effects of **B.C.E Ecclesia:** *In the Athens government, the ecclesia was a critical institution that played a central role in the political life of the city. The Ecclesia had the power to nominate and elect magistrates who were responsible for administering the city's affairs and carrying out the decisions of the assembly. The Ecclesia also had the authority to pass laws and to decide on issues related to foreign policy, defense, and the administration of justice. Ecclesia was responsible for establishing an agenda for its meetings, and any citizen could propose a matter for discussion. The Athenian assembly would then vote on the proposal and if it passed, it would become a law or policy. In addition to its legislative powers, The Ecclesia also participated in the judicial process in Athens. The Ecclesia members would try cases involving serious crimes such as murder and they* *could impose punishment. This made it an important institution for ensuring justice and upholding the rule of law in the city. (Study.com)*

Let me remind you of something based on the definition of The Ecclesia that I just stated. The Greek city-states of that time established all their government, including the **Athenian Boule** and **Solon's** era groups that worked along with the Ecclesia. The Greek philosophers and the logic of their philosophies that they had earned, and other places formed in the Greek city-states helped establish the governments and the rule of law. As we defined earlier, with the definition or the number, the two definitions of what the post power would be, you saw a statement of secular and non-secular. This example of the Ecclesia from the BCE era is the exact example of secular power. However, a source of power was missing from the Greek city-states. This particular power was the well-established non-secular power, which I titled in the earlier parts of the book; Greek Hellenistic Gumbo. But what was happening now was that the Romans would adopt the same philosophies and repeat what had been done 500 years before its existence as an empire, and they would reinstate this but as a Greek/Roman Hellenistic gumbo. The Greek Hellenistic Gumbo. The ecclesia was not successful in its implementation because it had a big issue, and the issue that it was having did not have the spiritual part. That will be encapsulated within it. The Romans would correct that issue when they created their Greek Roman Hellenistic Jambalaya, and this would be done in the form of establishing a secular. But with the initial powers being in the non secular, which the Greeks or the Romans did not control, that power lay within *India, Persia, and Egypt's spiritual Buddhist, Magi & hm-ntr priesthood temple NON-SECULAR systems*. I will not go too far with that as now, but just to give you somewhat of an idea as we proceed forward, and you will see how this whole God's economic system is going to come together. But in my conclusion, I will give you pretty much the whole layout from how I see it, and I will give you the information so you can research and discern it for yourself. But don't get lost right here. Remember that The Ecclesia of B.C.E was a secular form of government, and I described it as the Greek Hellenistic gumbo. But now there will be another creation that is the same thing as the Ecclesia Concept. Reimplemented, but under only one philosopher's logic, the Aristotelian.

I'm going to list several names and events below. You should familiarize yourself with these personalities and events, even if not in depth. Maybe a 20- to 30-minute search on these names and events will give you a decent basis to move forward with the timeline that I'm about to display. The reason I feel an in-depth understanding in the beginning is not needed for what I'm about to describe eventually in the rest of this chapter. This just for the sole purpose of you seeing what the Greek Ecclesia's government and those that were responsible for helping put these things in place, how it is going to repeat in the Roman Republic and eventual empire. These names will give you an understanding of the different codes of law that were established at the beginning of the idea. Of property rights. Then, there will be a war between the patricians and the plebeians. That is called the conflict of orders.

Draco the Lawgiver: Drakon, circa 625. To circa 600 BCE. *Also called drako or drakon according to Athenian tradition, was the first legislator of Athens in ancient Greece. He replaced the system of oral law and blood feud with the draconian Constitution (The draconian Code.), a written code to be enforced. A court of law. (Wikipedia)*

Solon, born Circus, 630 BCE, died circa 560 BCE. *He was the Athens statesman known as one of the Seven Wise Men of Greece. Solon ended exclusive aristocratic control of the government, substituted a system of control by the wealthy, and introduced a new and more humane law code. He is one of the major figures of classic antiquities. Code of laws of Solon* **([Property Laws including Human property]).** *(Britannica.)*

The Conflict of the Orders, or the Struggle of the Orders *(redefining and expanding Property Law [marriage, wife, children & slaves, where male citizen property rights are extended to lower classes as PRIVILEGES to be included by law; Public. not hereditary aristocratic right: Private]) was a political struggle between the plebians, commoners, and the patricians, aristocrats of the ancient Roman Republic, lasting from 50 BCE to 287 BCE (Wikipedia).*

Again, I would like to remind the reader that the Greeks bought Greece was not, as we understand it today, as a country. These were Greece or Greek city-states. They were not in one complete state. As we know, the definition of a state today is a country. These were city-states functioning as individual countries, and the governing governments of these countries function today. Also, take the time to note that Alexander the Great and the time he started his wars of conquest, exactly where he conquered, and after his death, where were the three generals that he had at the time that became heads of state of what countries? Then you will notice that these countries were the center of all education and knowledge from their spiritual systems or temples as we call it today. Each one of these countries and their spiritual systems had existed for millennia. Then I would request a quick search of the names of the different Greek philosophers we know. Today and find out what their actual philosophies were, and you may find out some interesting things that a number of these philosopher's philosophies came from these countries that these generals had taken over after the death of Alexander the Great.

This work is purposely a very short study or a short read, something may say, but it's imperative as we proceed in this last chapter. For you to familiarize yourself with the things that I've pointed out to you stated above. The earliest seven chapters were to give you a part of my philosophy and give the historical precedence for It. But in this chapter, we're making a timeline because it will take so many, so, so many pages, and we'll make it a much longer read. But a lot of this you must do yourself. Just like I said, familiarize yourself with it because you will see a pattern moving forward. This pattern will explain the rest of what I told you in the other seven chapters. I can also help you see that this is a repeat of the Greek Hellenistic gumbo. Then, you will understand what the Donation of Constantine was all about. This will give you a profound understanding of the difference between secular and non-secular and how this came to produce the economic system we have today and experienced. For millennia, it was based on a spiritual **PRIVATE** non secular left and a physical/worldly secular **PUBLIC** right of what would become an accounting sheet or two separate sides of an accounting ledger.

Now that the table has been set for the display of the different theologians who gave Aristotelian logic to what was set in motion for the next 1000 years, I believe we're experiencing an economy and system of government that I will start by giving you a few quotes from a number of these theologian scholars.

While theologians agreed that one did not need to be ordained to preach indulgences. pardons, after all, were not sacraments which only priests could administer. Rather, remissions pertained to the church's keys of jurisdiction, not the key of order: **The keys are twofold, namely of orders and of jurisdiction. The key of orders is a kind of sacrament; And since sacrament's effects are not determined by man, but by God, the priest cannot assay the amount of due punishment which has been remitted in the form of Conscience Though the key of orders; Rather so much is remit as God has ordained. But the key of jurisdiction is not sacrament, and its effect is subject to man's decisions: And the** *effect of this key is the remission which is had through indulgences. As such, remission does not pertain to the dispensing of sacraments but to the dispensing of the common goods of the church, and so even non-priests who are delegated can grant [that is publicized] indulgences. (Promissory notes on the treasury of merits. Page 30.)*

Evolution of the implementation of jurisdiction by spiritual example of the keys to justify the Greek Ecclesia reintroduction of the Patrician Era reducing the Plebeians to privilege by law only on the secular side.

The word redemption itself implies a buyback (re-d-emptio), The verb from which the noun derives, (Redimere), refers to ransoming off captives and slaves. Scriptures and the Liturgy frequently invoked the metaphor. The Psalm is lamented that Yahweh had sold his people for no price (Psalms 43: 13) In the New Testament, Saint Paul wrote to the Corinthians that their freedom from the slavery of sin had been brought at a great price. (I Corinthians 6: 20) and Peter recalled the redemption came not from "Corruptible" things as gold or silver... but from the precious blood of Jesus. First Peter 1: 18 to 19. And of course, Jesus's blood was precious because it was the price (pretium In Latin, both words have the same etymology of humanity's salvation. Patristic (Era) stories highlighted the biblical imagery. Jerome discussed Jesus as the price of humanity's redemption from the slavery of sin. Augustine called him the good merchant who purchased men and women to be the slaves of God, a blessed bondage. The medieval liturgy of the church as well as the religious drama of the High Middle Ages continually reinforce these biblical and patristic images.

*The combination of these historical developments came on the 27th of January 1343, when Pope Clemens VI (1342- 52) Proclaim the Bull **Unigenitus**, bull intended to announce the Jubilee observance of 1350. In the introduction to this Decretal, Clemens laid out the scriptural basis for both jubilees and indulgences. The Messianic law had provided that all debts be cancelled every 50 years; The Church eagerly extended the same generosity in an invitation of I Peter 1: 18 to 19 the pope talk that Jesus. Roth, the redemption of the human race, not through the blood of goats and of calves, which were the sacrifices of the old law, nor by the "corruptible gold and silver. Rather he redeemed his by the precious blood of that pure and immaculate lamb." In the great act of salvation, the sacrifice innocent shed no small drop of blood on the altar of the cross." **(Promissory Notes on the Treasury of Merit, page 26.)***

You will find that all the keywords related to the **process of salvation describe a financial transaction** in which we freely agree to place ourselves under jurisdiction of said agreement of sin-based debt, they give this debt value, and then it's **underwritten** by the secular, which in turn charges back to the Treasury of Merit for a debit issued to the debt holder that accepted the debt.

Wishing to store a treasury for the sons of his Holy Father, such that there might now be an infinite treasure for men through which those who draw upon it are made friends of God. Indeed, this treasury is not wrapped in cloth nor hidden in a field but committed to be dispense to the faithful profitably through Saint Peter, the bearer of the keys of heaven, and to his successor on earth, and applied mercifully, for right and reasonable causes to the truly penitent and confessed now for the plenary, now for the partial remission of temporal penalties owed for sin.

Pope Clement recall that the great spilling of Christ blood had won for the church militant, the church triumphant having no need of it and an inexhaustible fund of merit; to which were added those of the Blessed Mother and of all the martyrs and Saints throughout history. Penitence in a state of grace, as in the words of Clement, the theologians generally, those who were remade into friends of God because they had made a valid confession and receive the grace of absolution in the sacrament of penance could make withdrawals from the treasury for the payments of spiritual debts. (Notes on the Treasury of Merit, pages 27- 28.)

Consequently, they describe indulgences as payments from the churches and exhaustible treasury of merit. Bonaventure taught that" remissions or indulgences are granted from the superabundant merits which belong to the Church, which indeed are, onto its spiritual treasury." The Aristotelian Thomas Aquinas called the treasury of merit the formal cause of pardons:" Indeed, the cause of remission of penalty in indulgences is nothing other than the abundance of merits of the Church." The Church **underwrote spiritual promissory notes** good for a penitent's outstanding debt of sin. The metaphor of the treasury, in turn, encouraged the comparison between SPIRITUAL DEBITS AND CREDITS. The canonist **Hostiensis** taught that:

The Martyrs shared their blood for the faith and the church, and they were punished beyond that for which they had sinned. It so occurs that in Christ shedding of blood all sins is punished, and this effusion of blood is the stored treasury in the casket of the church, of which the church possesses the keys. Hence, when the church wishes, she is able to open the chest and will be able to grant to any her treasury by granting pardons and remissions to the faithful. (Promissory notes on the treasure of merit.)

Thomas Aquinas also compared "accounts":

The Superabundant account of the merit of Christ and his saints exceeds the needs of all penitent sinners throughout all of history. Withdrawals, no matter how frequent or how great, could never bankrupt or empty the Treasury of Merit.

Numerous scholars have condemned the authentic and mercantile imagery of indulgence in the Middle Ages as spiritually bankrupt and desiccated. The imagery of the Treasury, however, was not only rooted in the economic and social conditions of the High Middle Ages but was deeply scriptural and therefore Christian. (Promissory Notes on the Treasury of Merit, page 25.)

These philosophies became Canon law and a significant part of the fabric of the Society of its time. And there was no more apparent than this statement right here:

All men are spiritually equal in Christ. Doesn't imply that they should be socially equal in the world. **(The Origins and Development, Vol 1, page 695.)**

Pena = Debt: becomes the basis of **commerce** that will be exported and imposed on the world, but God had to create another world known as the New World.

Peter the Chanter summed these up well: "*We say, therefore, that this pardon is conferred on body and soul when these three are present, namely, the authority of the church, the communion of suffrages, and the work and devotion of the penitent.*"

Indulgence could only be valid after interior conversion had prompted such regret for sin that the penitent sought absolution in sacrament confession. That change of heart, as well as the grace infused in the sacrament of Penance, made a penitent fit to receive the benefits of an indulgence. Otherwise, pardons simply had no validity, as in the teachings of Peter the Chanter.

Peter of Poitiers (c. 1130-1205) likewise argued in his **Sententiarum Libri Quinque**, that the validity of alms indulgences depended upon the purity of penitent intentions, not the amount of money contributed:

a rich man should give the same sum of money as a very poor old woman, should he believe that he gets as much remission as her? Nonsense!... For God does not ask of a man what he is unable to do; He does not consider how much is given, but.... From what intention?

Full atonement for sin, they argue, required both confession and sacrament, absolution of sin, and the completion of the penance imposed thereafter. Both confession and penance were necessary because each serious sin incurred both guilt (CULPA) And penalty (PENA, for instance, in English called "debt"). In the sacraments of penance, a merciful God forgave the guilty of sins so serious as to condemn their Perpetrated to an infernal eternity. God's justice, however, which required that restitution be made, had not yet been satisfied restitution could be made through. The completion of penitential works, either those imposed by confessors or other works taken up as the Initiative of the penitent, such as indulgences. This remitted the penalty or debt of sin that remained after confession. Since the salvation of the soul began with a valid reception of the sacraments of penance.

__Franciscan Bonaventure__ offers that Satisfactory penance constitutes two benefits. These two are medicine against future sins and the price of counseling. The debt of sin. __Thomas Aquinas__ agreed with Bonaventure. Explanation: Satisfactory penance is said to serve two ends, namely the solution of debt and as medicine for avoiding sin. In the labor which they required of the repentant indulgence and discipline, both mind and body. To be eligible for indulgence, the proposed work must serve the Christian Commonwealth. As Peter the Chanter asserted: pardon is granted for the necessity of a sacred place or a handicapped Penitent or for the relief of the Holy Land and Jerusalem.

Finally, the prelates of the Church indulgence may publicly useful building projects. The sources record many remissions for bridges and road repair for medieval people well appreciated their value as symbols of humankind, humankinds spiritual journey, and the maintenance and construction of roads. Bridges were considered works of mercy for the relief of travelers and pilgrims. As an anonymous 13th-century theologian of Metz argued __(Promissory notes on the treasury of merits: paragraphs above included.; pages 14,15,16, and 17.)__

I have disclosed several paragraphs of several of the great minds of the 11th, 12th and 13th-century theologians as they debated and eventually became Canon law in the hierarchy of the actual Ecclesia Catholic Church. These minds debated and placed into action what became adopted by the church of the on goings and functioning of the church. Within this economic structure that profited the church greatly at the expense of sinners that would become, unbeknownst to them, debtors. Please do keep in mind all these structures that I'm pointing out because these structures would be exported globally. A structure that would bring the entire globe under the subjection of these ideals and funding;

what would become a powerful economic system unimaginably profitable under the description of a newly discovered world that would be created by law. Which was, in my opinion, not based in reality but found in the documents of what we come to know today as the **Doctrine of Discovery** which is an elaboration of one of what I consider the most dangerous documents ever created in the mind of man and made law that subjugated the world called, **The Great Charter:** *the Magna Carta*. This concept would be rehashed repeatedly within the many countries that would be relabeled as states.

Now, let us return to the **TWO KEYS** one is God\ private (Left side.) The second key is jurisdiction\ public. (Right side.) Initially, the order was God, king, but there must be three remember. Father, Mother, and Son that became Father, Son, and Holy Ghost. The feminine was hidden in the Patrician era because she became property. But most important is her power as a pass-through of all blessings as the facilitator of all God's gifts in this world and universe needed to be owned to place in eternal servitude all that God passed through her through the verbal description of Papal Edicts *hereditary servitude*. Regardless of how you name or clarify it, there are 1-2 and three of any form of creation on earth or anywhere in this universe are Father, Mother, and Son = seed, gestation, and genesis. As above, so below. This is eternal repetition. 1-2 and three. God, King only equals 1 and 2......Anything you are trying to create must have the feminine principle, or you cannot produce anything from the spiritual into the physical or manifestation. 1-2 and three. 1 spiritual/ soul, 2 spiritual/manifestation, and 3 physical/ existence or the body. One and two are not subject to anything physical as three, which represents existence in the body (the physical world). God's protection is on one and two, but two must give birth to three, right? So now you get the theory of **The Divine Right**. God now gives the divine right (Protection) to the sovereign kings (Secular.) Which holds the two keys of jurisdiction by the authority of God (God in this instance and the one stated above in this idea is indicated in the description of several papal bulls as the papal office or the Holy See as God's representation on earth. So, therefore, the vicar with the power of God, which has already been stated by several 11th, 12th, and 13th-century theologians.) No, God cannot touch or exist in the physical without contamination of the soul or pure form. The soul puts on a protection suit called the spirit to interact with the body or world. My point, God, as 1 created 2 the king (As the feminine vassal to give birth or pass through a new entity). The king was empowered by God (The Holy See) created 3: A New World.

(Now, within this New World, the Holy See represents God recognized by law in this New World.) Now, the accounting sheet; Left side: God/ soul: assets and debits. The dividing line: King/spirit; pass through the holder of accounts or arbiter. Right side: New World/physical (: created by Law) l: liability, debts, and credits.

I humbly ask you to pray for me as I attempt to show you a very elaborate structure that was put together over 2000 years, but a replica of that which existed before on the secular side. This structure is much more complete. With encapsulation of the non-secular and secular for the creation of a New World. However, this New World would follow the law of creation. From spiritual to physical form of manifestation.

It is important that I now give you an understanding of two terms that are going to be very important in putting this whole picture. Or structured together. The first will be the **Donation of Constantine,** and the second will be **Petra Penance**. However, I think it is imperative that you take your time and go back and understand the **Conflict of Orders**. This will go a long way into helping you understand the beginning of Rome as a Republic up until it became an empire, but you will get an opportunity to see the overlapping structure from the Greeks. This is so important because it will explain pretty much everything to you, and you will see it within 250 or so years. How the structure of everything a government and society came together even until today, and how things are basically identically the same through this ideology of laws and privilege. But just as a simple example, I will give you the orders of **Patrician, Privileged, Plebeian, and Slaves (Slaves as in the form of property.)**

The donation of Constantine is the basis of everything in the ecclesial enterprise that is about to be formed. Within my observation, Petras Penance will be the account in which payments will be made as insurance from sovereign kings to protect their inheritance or land. The Holy See becomes a form of actual global insurance or TRUST for kings to insure against being robbed, land and taken, etc., and Petra's Penance was your figurative monthly payment to God. Your insurance was a spiritual covering. Your land would be in *TRUST* and recorded by God, which no secular power could subject or challenge your *DIVINE RIGHT.* Allow me to now give you some historical context and examples of this structure: *Layman who contracted to make such payments surrendered their* lands to St. Peter or the Roman Church, received the usufructuary enjoyment of them and agreed to pay an annual sum in acknowledgment of the ownership of the lands by the Roman Church. The analogy between the instructions and the feudal organizations is also striking. The Pope was the Lord, and the holder of the lands was the vassal. Even in papal documents and terminologies of Lord and vassal was often employed and when the relationship was first established, the holders of such lands customarily rendered homage and fealty to the Pope. The Lord gave protection by means of spiritual censures instead of temporal weapons. The vassal was rendered financially in place of military service.

The layman who assumed this position were actuated by the desire to obtain the protection that could be given to them by the occupants of the See of St Peter. The Norman conquerors of northern Italy in the 11th century were seeking to be legitimate by Papal sanction, a position which rested solely upon the right of conquest. When Ramiro, King of Aragon, had failed in an attempt to deprive his brother, Ferdinand, of the Throne of Castile, He sought to protect himself against his brother's anticipated counterattack by becoming the vassal of the Apostolic See. He did this in 1063 before Gregory VII put forth the claim that all Christian rulers of Spain ought to do homage to the Apostolic See because the peninsula was part of the Donation of Constantine. The purpose of the Duke of Silesia is Patent in the letter which he wrote to the Pope in 1323. His brothers, he said, had ordered Peters penance to be levied in their lands as a recognition of their immediate subjugation to the Apostolic See,' pursuing faithfully that if any, by chance, any Emperor or King of Rome should wish to extend his jurisdiction over us, de facto we shall be defended from. His violence and injury by the protection of the Apostolic See.' The papacy sometimes claimed homage and fealty or tribute, but only when it had established a presumption that the land upon which the claims were made belonged to the Roman Church and had been or was tributary. When, for example, Gregory the 7th asserted the papal lordship over Spain on the basis of the donation of Constantine, he assumed that the census once paid from Spain had been suspended as a result of the conquest of the Saracens exceptions of this type was uncommon, and it may be assumed ordinarily that a payment of tribute was begun originally at the initiative of the lay Lord or ruler who desired the protection or moral. Sanction of the Apostolic See. **(Financial Relationships of the Papacy with England to 1327: pages 130- 131.)**

The Donation of Constantine became the basis of the agreements that this New World will be built around and the payment from the king or the sovereign that owned these lands would be through Petra's Penance. This theory was debated during the 11th, 12th, and 13th centuries of the establishment of it, but it was actually accepted in the 3rd, 4th, and 5th centuries through a number of different councils. Under this agreement, no one in the secular world or physical or should I say public world could take anything that God had given you therefore kings and sovereigns placed their lands in trust with the Apostolic See, no earthly power, king or otherwise, court of any nature, could take anything that God had given you. This included no form of deed, or no lien of any type could take away your property because it was entrusted to God, which is his. God's representation was the Apostolic See based on this theory, it being put in trust with the Apostolic See *this gave birth to the **Doctrine of The Divine Right** to rule on earth*, or should I say in legal terms, in this **New World** that I am about to begin to show you through the number of edicts. That is going to provide a legal basis for the conquest of land by the sovereign kings that bought into the enterprise, the Ecclesia Enterprise of the Apostolic See. Unbeknownst to most, the basis of this right would be put into place by law and the sighting of law through documentation written up in the form of edicts and other Apostolic See documents. The common name for this law book that I'm referring to is Named.: The Holy Bible.

The creation of the New World, literally following the exact operation and procedure of the Ecclesia Catholic Church And tithing to the Church through its ecclesia enterprise that under catechism of The Council of Trent gave the Greek word EKKLESIA that was solely secular, a religious definition to mean church or spiritual related. Just to expand it in order of operations vetted of the so-called non secular side....... Of hundreds of years of trial and error on the Greek secular side and via the donation of Constantine, the basis of uniting non secular and secular began to recreate the ecclesia spiritual enterprise following the philosophy of ancient times: as above, so below....... Again, 1-2 and three, however it created must exist first in the spiritual, then manifest in the physical. What I'm about to show you is the main non secular executive orders called edicts that gave the jurisdiction to create this New World, which would reflect the same structure and order of opportunity of the ecclesia enterprise from the spiritual left side via the pass-through of the columns of separation.......

Hold on because I'm about to baptize you into deep thought: Soul(left) Spirit (Column of Separation) Body/Manifestation/New World (Right). Now let's put this into practice: God (Left/ or Private) King/ Pass Through (Roman Column of Separation by Law or Privileges) New World (Right or Public).

Ecclesia enterprise would be duplicated on the public side as a form of franchise enterprise. Therefore, the order is, as above, so below: The Ecclesia enterprise and the franchised enterprise.

The Ecclesia Church (God) Ecclesia Enterprise (The King) Franchised Enterprise/ New World (Monarch): 1. Father 2. Son 3. Holy Spirit, the Holy Trinity, or the Holy Triangle? On the spiritual side, maybe? What would be non-secular?

Now let's go on and create the 2nd and 3rd triangles or trinities, maybe?

God= Ecclesia Church= King= Ecclesia Enterprise (Left side/ Private) = The Law= (The King as Monarch by Jurisdiction (Roman Column/ Roman Fasces that separates left & right sides). The de facto god of Creation by Manifestation of Created order by de facto Law: And god said," let there be......") New World= The Magna Carta (The Manifestation of the Right side/ Public, Sin, Debt & Servitude/ Slavery.)= The Charta/Charter= The State(Form of Franchised Enterprises)= Corporation (Chatter. Just not from a monarch but by INC, LLC, etc. from.: The State)

This is the structure. Now I'm going to give you God's law that created it. I'm going to give you the road map... You will have to arrive at the conclusion on your own.

I'm going to take you through this last half of the chapter fast. I don't plan to hold your hand on this. You're going to need to do a lot of this research on your own, but I have pointed you in the proper direction. I'm going to give you the name of the documents. Please don't take the statement of I'm not going to hold your hand as disrespect, but there's a lot to go over and for the sake of time and space and not trying to make this book too long. You're going to need to do these things and arrive at your own conclusion as stated above. After stating a number of these documents, I might give a short opinion on certain documents, but more of this will be in my conclusion.

1211: *The Pope grants Ireland to Henry*

*The intercession of John of Salisbury on behalf of the king persuaded the Pope to grant Ireland to Henry to be held as a **Fief (: and a state of land held on condition of federal service.)** from the Roman Church. The papal right to make the concession rested upon the forged Doctrine* *of Constantine, which was believed to confer upon the Roman Church the ownership of all islands. The Bull Laudabiliter, which is sometime assumed to have been the letter, is probably a forgery.*

When Henry did visit Ireland in 1171, he received the allegiance of the Anglo-Norman Barons and of some of the Irish leaders, Alexander the Third acknowledge the conquest reminded him of the special rights which the Roman Church had in islands; and urged him to conserve and extend those rights as far as they existed in Ireland and to establish any nonexistent rights which ought to be held and belong to the Roman Church. At the same time, the Pope wrote to the king's princess and clergy of Ireland recommending the acceptance of Henry in these letters neither fealty nor census was mentioned. Another letter purporting to have been written by Alexander the Third, which confirms Adrian's concession of Ireland saving an annual penny from each household to Saint Peter and the Roman Church is false. It therefore seems highly improbable that Henry the Second ever acknowledged the feudal lordship of the papacy over Ireland. (Financial relationships of the Papacy with England to 1327. William E Lunt.)

This is just some of the back story that led to what I'm about to disclose to you right now of the 1211 agreement.

Circumstances under which John surrendered England and Ireland to the Roman Church are, for the most part, well known. In 1211 Innocent the Third sent, apparently at John's request two envoys Pandolf and Duran to attempt a settlement of the quarrel which had begun between King and Pope in 1206 over the appointment of Stephen Langton to Archbishopric of Canterbury. When John refused to accept some of the conditions which the Pope wished to impose Pandolf pronounced him excommunicated declared his subject dissolved from his allegiances and announced that the Pope would send an army to England to exact John's deposition. Thereafter the king found that he could not rely upon the support of many of his English Barons. The coalition which John had built against France was weakened and it became apparent that Philip Augustus of France was projecting an invasion of England.

On the 27th of February 1213, Innocent the Third. Replied to a letter stating what the king must do to make his peace and obtain absolution. It contained no requirement of homage or fealty. Repeated the form of peace which Pandolf had born in 1211, but this may not have included all the conditions specified at that time since Pandolph then carried at least one other letter. Nothing indicates that fealty was demanded in 1211, however we have in the annals of Burton what purports to be a verbatim report of the conversation between

John and Pandolf in 1211. Pandolf, whom Innocent the Third sent to see that John fulfilled the terms of the letter of 1213, met the king at Dover on the13th of May. On his way through France, Pandolf had suspended, pending the result of his negotiation with John, the invasion of England projected by Philip Augustus at the invitation of the Pope. At the interview with the nuncio John accepted the papal requirements, ratifying his act by the oath of four barons and by letters announcing it on the 15th of May. John issued a charter granting Innocent and his successors, the kingdoms of England and Ireland, to be received back and held by the grantor in vassalage of God and the Roman Church. He professed to act voluntarily for the purpose of obtaining the remission of his sin because he said he have offended God and our Holy Mother Church and many things, and we are known to be most needful of Divine Mercy. Therefore, nor can we offer anything worthy for proper satisfaction to God and the Church. Unless we humiliate ourselves and our kingdoms for the act, he claimed to have the council of his Barons and acknowledgement of the relationship thus created, he swore fealty to the Pope in the presence of Pandolf according to the form of oath given in the charter, and undertook a perpetual obligation to pay annually for all service and Custom 1000 marks saving to him and his heirs their jurisdiction, privileges and Regalian rights. 700 marks were from England and 300 for Ireland. The whole sum was to be paid in equal parts at Easter and Michaelmas each year. The charter was attested by 13 lay and ecclesiastical bearings. On the 3rd of November 1213, Innocence the Third accepted the gift, took John, his heirs and his Kingdom under the protection of himself and Saint Peter, and ceded the Kingdom of John and his successors in fear. On 3rd October 1213, John and performed homage before Nicholas, Bishop of Tusculum, who had recently come to England as Papal Legate. At that time, he issued a more formal copy of his charter, sealed with a golden bull and on the 21st of April 1214, Innocent the Third repeated his letter of acceptance. (Financial Relationships of the Papacy with England to 1327. Pages 133, 134, 135, and 136.)

I would ask that the reader pay attention to the number of countries mentioned, but it appeared that the Barons of those countries were very influential in getting or exercising a lot of the rights that the Pope claimed that he had over those lands based on the donation of Constantine. But earlier in the quotes that I made, you have seen that they called the donation of Constantine as well as the demand for payment to Saint Peter and the Roman Church as possible forgeries. Yet and still, you see that I went on to show that these acts were statements of forgeries and that they were not some type of scheme. They were being acted out by kings. I would also ask that the reader pay attention and remember the statement with the Donation of Constantine that guaranteed St. Peter and the Roman Church the lordship or ownership of all lands or islands.

1213: *The Magna Carta (The Great Charter)*

June 15, 1215, was the actual date of the signing of the Magna Carta. I often like to refer to the year 1213 as the Magna Carta because of everything that happened within that year that led up to the foundation of what would become the Great Charter of the Magna Carta. Once reflecting on the history of 1213, you will end the disagreement between King John and the Papacy. You will find that the agreement that King John signed and voluntarily submitted himself and the rights of England and Ireland over to the papacy. You will see that that agreement did not allow King John to enter in any other agreement, and if he did, he would forego his hereditary rights for himself as well as his lineage to his Regalian privileges. After that date it is somewhat disputed, but there is some recorded record that states that King John stated that he did not sign over all these rights in the presence of the Barons that were in England and that he may have done it under some form of duress. From some of the reading I have done, it has also suggested that some of the Barons revolted against him once they found out that he gave over all this authority to the Pope and the office of the papacy. If you look at the history of this whole interaction, you will find that they started to challenge King John and King John under fear of basically being overthrown by the Barons, went to the papacy for help. The Barons caused King John to submit to another agreement and that agreement is known today and by history as the Magna Carta. The issue with this agreement is that under the 1213 agreement that King John had signed with the actual Pope, he did not have the authority or jurisdiction to sign anything over or make any agreements concerning England or Ireland on the behalf of those countries outside of the authorization of the actual unit owner under that agreement, which was the Pope. Now I'm going to list three different documents below and the dates of these documents that you can look up and you can see more. I first must warn you that the first documents, the first two documents, are what set up the power of the third actual document of 1217. That will create what we have stated above, which I believe is classified as the New World.

1215: The Magna Carta
1217: Carta De Foresta
1217: Inns of Court

This is where the Ecclesia Enterprise creates the law. Then by this law the king, which is the sovereign, is redefined on the right side as the monarch. And under the power of the jurisdiction of the law on the right side, which is given its power by the ecclesia enterprise on the left side, empowers the new entity called the monarch, in which the king from the left side can interact with the secular side on the right side in the body of the entity of the monarch, which creates a New World. This New World is reflected in the document called the Magna Carta. This document creates the actual charter, which will be known later as corporations within this New World. That gives birth to the other two documents of the year 1217. The Magna Carta created the actual jury system that we use today, and the second document as stated above, takes away basically property rights and puts it under the power of the actual charter/future corporation. But understand these are all separate entities and powered by this ecclesia enterprise. Which is nothing but a way to collect funds or to create what's on the left side, on the actual right side and expressed this power through a secular law system that is closely created off of the ways that the Ecclesia Law functions on the left side. But for the purpose of taxing on the right side as well as what the ecclesia does on the left side. However, the left side, which is the side that God resides on, which is non secular, cannot contaminate itself by interacting with the right side, which is a corporal world and secular so it must have a separation. As I stated throughout this whole book, following the ancient description of the cycles of creation: as above, so below. The three entities created through the years of 1215 to 1217 as stated above, is the foundational government of the New World that will be the buttress of God's law that will enslave the world. As I stated before, 1,2, and 3 represent the documents above. Now what? We will go on to show you how the next three are created. But first let's show you the breakdown of the system that will bring about the creation of all of these franchises; or should I refer to them, everyone or everything that exists in this New World as Franchised entities.

Now let us give an understanding of what the Inns of court consist of that was founded in 1217, or should I say the 13th century. This institution or number of institutions will become the force multipliers that the only responsibility is to exact God's Law on this newly developed New World and enforce the tax that will be returned to God in the same format in which you seen that King John of England had to pay unto St. Peter and the Roman Church. *(Method of Levy: The tribute was ordinarily levied by the general collector of papal revenue during the short periods when no general collector was present in England. If the Apostolic See was occupied, the Pope usually notified the king to whom the tribute should be paid. In 1233, the agents were the factors of a FIRM of Italian MERCHANTS, and in 1236, the agents were a papal Chamberlain. Even when a collector was residing in the kingdom, the Pope might ask the king to deliver the tribute to the Treasury of the TEMPLE OF LONDON, to a FIRM of Camara MERCHANTS or to a legate or nuncio other than the collector. The king might send the money to the Papal Camara by his own messengers if he preferred, and he often chose this method when the renderer of the sum due for the tribute was preliminary to a royal request of papal favors;. Financial relationships of the Papacy with England to 1327.)*

History of the Inns of Court of London.

In 1218, Pope Honorius III issued a papal bull prohibiting Roman Clerk Catholic clergy from practicing law in secular courts. In the 13th century, laymen began teaching law and law guilds, which eventually became London's Inns of Court. In the 14th century, lawyers lived and worked in the temple and area of London. In 1337, the area was divided into the Inner Temple and the Middle Temple. The Lincolns Inn can track its records back to 1422, and the Grays Inn is able to track its records back to 1569. (Study.com)

*The Inns of Court are four institutions in England and Wales that were established in the 13th century; The Inns are responsible for getting individuals to practice law. The four Inns are the Grays Inn, the Lincolns Inn, the Inner Temple and the Middle Temple. The Inns are located in central London near the Royal Courts of Justice, a grade one listed building that is located in Westminster and houses the Minister's High Court of Justice in England and the Court of Appeals in England and Wales. The Inns of court have three Grades of membership, students, barristers, also known as lawyers and benchers. Which are masters of the bench **(Bench in Italian: PANCA= BANC = BANK)** the governing body of the Four Inns consists of benchers; The senior bencher is the treasurer, which is the leader of the governing body. (**Study.com.)***

I would also like to note that whenever there is a hearing that's called with several judges that come together to decide a case, it's called an **EN BANC** hearing. I also think it's important to point out that all judicial hearings before the creation of the Magna Carta were by Canon law, which is ecclesia law that was judged, or hearings were held by bishops or Cardinals of the church. If there were ever an issue of undecided Canon law, there would be councils that were called together that will consist of. Several bishops or cardinals from a certain region decide the law concerning the Ecclesia Canon law but of course this would be on the left side. But since there was a creation on the right side, which would be secular, and the left side is non secular, with these hearings, the exact thing would be duplicated, except there would be judges instead of bishops or cardinals, and the hearings would be called En Banc Sessions.

Now let me give you a little more on the other 1217 decision concerning the Yeoman people.

The root of the Holocaust against the white Yeomanry of Britain lies in the history of the land swindles perpetrated against them in the late 12th and early 13th century, as the Lords obtained their rights against the king as formalized in the Magna Carta, they used them to expropriate the land rights of the Yeomen by means of the writ Of Novel Disseisin And what historian Rodney Hilton described as other "Lawyers traps" ownership was transferred to the Lords. People were allowed to remain on the ancestral land with something akin to a sharecropper status (or feudalistic Tax.)

Thomas Muir had been arrested for the crime of advocating the right to vote for white working men. At his trial, Braxfield ruled that Mr. Muir might have known that no attention could be paid by Parliament to such a rabble (the white worker who had petitioned for voting rights). What right have they to representation? A government in every country should be just like a corporation, and in this country, it is made up of land interests. Which alone has the right to be represented.

Once land the source of the independence of Britain, Yeoman, had been removed. The resulting dependency is attached to the white poor. The station of servility a process whose groundwork had been laid with juridical defense of ancestral peasant lands claims as a result of the establishment of the concept of villein tenure in the 12th century, the consequences of which eviction and enclosure. (They were white, and they were slaves. Page 20 and 21.)

I think it is important to understand that all these documents that have been stated earlier are actual legal documents. The additional documents that I will move on to state will be actual edicts given by the pope will be the basis of philosophy. Or legal philosophy that will be discerned in these Inn of courts and made into secular law. The next thing that I believe is vital is you will start to see the creation of additional bibles. That will start to come out in other languages outside of the Italian language. Let us make a note that as New World franchises begin to move around the world under the documents which I will point out, that will lay the foundation of the doctrine of discovery. The prerequisite would be that the bible would be forced on to all these nations that were being conquered or through conquest, but the bible would be taught and ingrained into the populations. Within my opinion, these bibles were nothing more than the buttress or the beginning form of law, or the Book of Law on the ecclesial side that would come. To support the law on the secular side I will present to you now a document of 1302 written by Pope Boniface VIII, which is the exact example of how you would see a legal document today written up, but inside of this Pope's document, you will see him citing scripture from the bible as the basis to support his Edict. The only difference today or in legal documents today, and even back then after the legal system was created, its documents would be written up but citing law which is representative of the secular side.

1302 Unun Sanctum: *every human created to be subjects of the Roman Pontiff.*

Now, as I proceed forward, I'm going to give you three additional documents that I believe will understand all the buttress of the Doctrine of Discovery that was used to expand these franchises under God's law that had been established.

I think it is also important to understand that these groups signed on to this Ecclesia Enterprise to create more franchises around the world the different East and West Indian companies and the Dutch companies that popped up around the world. But I also started to see how the term CROWN started to be used oftentimes. You will start to see in some of the documentation the English crown, the Spanish crown, and the Dutch crown. Seeing that in this New World, everything was entities or enterprises, it started to appear as if the term crown, whether it's Spanish, English, or Dutch. It was really the reflection of maybe another corporation, maybe, I don't know.

1455: Romanus Pontifex: *This document gave birth to the doctrine of discovery and gave authorization to Christian countries to go out* *and basically expand their domination over the world, along with a document of 1452 introduced a new form of legal description for slavery, hereditary servitude was entered into the legal description.*

*1481: **Aeterni Regis**: Pope Sixtus to resolve a dispute between Portugal and Spain created this edict giving Portugal land yet to be discovered alone. Africa's West Coast and Guinea to Portugal.*

*1492-93: **Dudum Siquidem**: This document expands the juris- diction of slavery or enslavement to the Americas and justifies the colonization and enslavement of Africans.*

The Chartered Corporations was, of course, known to English law. The oldest corporations, the universities, the churches, and the Inns of Court, however, were corporations by prescription or ancient usage well into the 19th century. Corporation corporate charters were jeal- ously guarded privileges because, in accordance with prior usage and theory, a charter carried with it not only corporate existence but also a monopoly of trade in a restricted class of merchandise. The market area this conceptual connection continued in England well into the 19th century. (Limited liability in historical perspective, page 13.)

I think it is important to be clear on the first three documents of the 12th century. These documents put in place an actual legal system on the right side, which is the secular side and which. All the actions duplicated throughout the history of the left side, which is the Ecclesia Church Canon Law side would be crossed over or pass through to another world, which we have classified as the New World. This is the sole purpose for creating these three documents. This followed the 11th century of different Aristotelian theologians creating a philosophy that matched what would be- come law on the right side, which is reflected in the top documents of the 12th century. The definition stated above, basically given the history of corporations but from an ancient historical perspective, indicates and fully describes the description and the actions. The first forms of corporations were churches, universities, and Inns of Court. Note that the Inns of Court is the beginning of this overall corporate system or charter system being placed on the right side.

Pope Honorius of 1218 gave instructions for any of the clergy or people within the church on the secular side that said they were not permitted to practice law on the secular side. For this reason, and for this reason only, within my opinion, it was to make sure that this new side that had been created that was the secular side, could not be as they would say in accounting or in banking, could not be Co-mingled with the left side, which was the private side, Ecclesia Church. No one from the left side, the private side, the ecclesia church side, or should I say the ecclesial enterprise side could Co-mingle with the right side, the public side, the secular side, the side that would basically become a mirror of the left side, which would be a form of franchising. The definition above also shows that charters were guarded very carefully because they were a form of monopoly. That's because, again, it was a repeat of the ecclesial side once you became an ecclesial church or a Catholic ecclesial church that was a form of franchise, and they set up franchises throughout the regions in what would become Europe. All these Catholic ecclesial enterprise churches would be under the control of the one church, which would be based in the Roman Church. As stated in that definition, it was a monopoly the hundreds of years that were taken to wipe out all other forms of churches or Arianism from the powerful African Bishop named Arius. This was to ensure that monopoly was put in place but based on what will be understood as the Roman Church. Now, what we will see in the creation of this New World that exists will be nothing but following the same principles that were carried out on the left side by the church, even with how legal cases and everything else would be decided, as well as the ancient forms and definitions of corporations. This would be governed by the individuals that were trained in these universities or Temples of London.

There should be no mistake made about it that this New World, from these legal documents of the 12th century, was started in Europe by what we would come to know as Europeans. All the treaty agreements were put in place for those who signed on to the edicts of the Popes of that day would be recognized within the second set of documents of the 1400s, when what had been created in the European concept or European continent would now be exported around the world. Under the same structure as the Ecclesia Church on the left side and governed by the concept of the Magna Carta of 1215. Yeah, let there be no mistake, the initial agreement that was done of 1213 was done between the Pope and the sovereign King John of that date. The actual document that was done in 1215 was between the Barons and the so-called sovereign King John. The first example of the 1213 document between King John and the Pope reflected the agreement between, let's say, God and the sovereign. 1215 was the document between what the law would create as the monarch and what would become entities of corporations but then named barons. In my opinion, and this is solely my opinion, The Inns Of Court were developed to protect the interests of collecting the tax for the actual monarch, which was in the body of the sovereign for the payments that had to go to Saint Peter's Roman Church, but also in the interests of the Barons To protect the privileged rights that had been won by them from King John and would be duplicated. As you can see from the document stated above, there were barons in every single region of what would become European states. The 1302 document done by Pope Boniface VIII set up what would become the year of 1400 documents that would be produced that allowed the European countries, which were Christian or Catholic countries to go out in the world and reduce all lands and people into servitude of the Catholic Church. The 1302 document done by Pope Boniface VIII is what set the precedence saying that all people. Then there's some that questioned the word Indies as in West Indies that the word Indies actually described people and saying all people are to be placed in the servitude of the Catholic Church. We understand servitude means the same as the definition, which is given in the 1452 and 1455 edicts, which were legal documents. Saying that the Christian or Catholic nations had the right to go into the world to reduce all infidels or to reduce all into hereditary servitude, which we would come to find out really meant slavery. This servitude or slavery would be referred to as a blessed servitude to Saint Peter's Roman Church. I'm going to move forward now and describe a very short overview of what this world, New World, would end up or entail and exactly how it came into the picture and this will be through the eyes of the vehicle which the Catholic Church labels servitude that we came to understand as slavery. For the record, I would like to state before I even start to describe that every class of human being, every ethnic group of human being was enslaved by someone or enslaved by their own people?

The same Christian nations will become European countries. They were a colonizing society. They conquered wards and enslaved each other throughout their entire history. Therefore, the philosophy that would be released on the world was nothing more than their normal culture, but now the world would be introduced to it and, in some cases, victimized by it. But again, I will reiterate everything they did to the world, they were doing to each other first. By stating this, that's the only thing that I'm trying to impress upon is the subject that I'm about to enter is not about slavery. I'm not here to debate the rights and wrongs of slavery. I'm not here to debate whether slavery was something that did something more to one race or type of person than the other. I'm just stating that it was a foundational part of human culture and societies of ancient times and as well as the current times that we're speaking about as dated above. My purpose for touching on the subject of slavery is it's a financial component that was created for the purpose of income or commerce in this New World and amongst all of the vehicles of earning and forms of ways of being taxed from the ecclesia church and after the ecclesia church the monarch as payments that had to go to the ecclesia church for the monarchs or the sovereigns right acting through the entity of the monarch to have the right or divine right to rule. As stated above, and the example between the Pope and King John and what he had to pay annually and the different patterns or different sources through which he had to pay his tribute, or should I say Ecclesia tax? Also, I would like to note that within this agreement that he made with the Pope, it gave him the privilege. I will reiterate this word privilege to his Regalian Rights; Right to rule as sovereign king through the body of entity of the monarch. Stated above, slavery was experienced by everyone, but what made this form of slavery different is the ancient forms of slavery were a form of prisoner of war. Also stated above, all these ancient forms of corporations were monopolies, and this was the ecclesia church version of corporations, which were executed through churches or how churches functioned as well as universities. So, once they organize under the form of the state, they also monopolize slavery. Slavery would no longer, or we could say servitude based on legal documentation of the 1400s, it would no longer be a privilege to everyone, and it was monopolized under the 1302 understanding of what Pope Boniface VIII described all people as being place under the servitude of the Catholic Church. So therefore, you can kind of say that this agreement pretty much created a form of trust, and this trust everything and everyone would be placed in this trust and all the fish, water, land, people, and memorials upon this world would be placed in the trust of the Ecclesia Church. Not to belabor the point any longer this monopolized form of slavery was under the guise of the description of these legal documents that all Christian countries and European countries signed we're given chartered agreements, which we understand chartered today as corporations. So, my point is this. Slavery was monetized by select groups of individuals for the purpose of commerce and commerce only. Therefore, the descriptions that I'm about to give concerning slavery, I will reiterate that it is not to debate whether right or

wrong because every human part of the human family has experienced it. My issue, which I'm about to point out, is the commerce
or the currency that basically benefited from the structure that I'm
trying to show you through historical patterns.

Now we have gone through over 2000 years of human history.
I have attempted to show you the patterns that I have observed
throughout this history through a plethora of very expensive
books, which if you take your time and look up some of these
books, you will see the expense that I incurred to obtain this
information. Now I plan to show you the true danger of the Magna
Carta or the Great Charter of 1215. As we go through these final
pages, I'm going to quote from a number of books that you guys
should consider purchasing, which will give you the whole layout
of this entire history based on the buttress that we have developed
right here within this book and you knowing the history. Please
do keep in mind there could be no Magna Carta without the
agreement of 1213 directly from King John to the actual pope. As I
stated before, I will continue to reiterate the old ancient statement
of, "as above, so below". Which is a meaning of the same way God
created the universe. Everything that goes up under that every
layer down is created with the identical same steps and this is
the same process that was used by the Ecclesia Church that was
learned from the ancient centers of wisdom and spirituality, which
Alexander the Great commandeered through the expression of his
generals that took over these three centers that were located in
Egypt, Persia and India. The Greeks made the mistake and handled
the secular part, but they could not rule the world. In which they
learn, but neglected initially from the Egyptians, Persians and
India. There must be a spiritual component which was labeled
non secular and these two must go together because whatever is
manifested on earth must first be manifested in heaven. The earth
or the physical is nothing but a reflection of the spiritual which in
all circumstances must be established first. So, this is why we must
pay attention to the agreement between the Pope and the King.
In the agreement of 1213, which gave birth to the Magna Carta
of 1215. Now proceeding forward, this agreement of the Magna
Carta of 1215 is what created the Inns of Court. Please make sure
you pay attention to this as we wrap this book up. Pay attention
to all the temples or the temples of London, these four houses
or institutions, is what created all of your basis of law anything
having to do with law? Judges, attorneys and lawyers, all these
different things are encapsulated within the Temple of London,

London. It is the center of all of this and this New World that was established. Everything that I'm doing and showing you what happened with the Magna Carta, which is reflective of England, is the same thing that was done in all of what would become the European states. Spain, Dutch so on and so forth. Pay attention to all the documents that were stated above, but I will pick up now from where I left off with the papal document of 1493.

*Pope issued in 1493 a series of papal bulls which established a line of demarcation between the colonial possessions of the two states: The East went to Portugal and the West went to Spain. The partitions, however, failed to satisfy Portuguese aspirations and in the subsequent year the contending parties reached a more satisfactory compromise in the Treaty of Tordesillas. Which ratified the papal judgment to permit Portuguese ownership of Brazil neither the papal arbitration nor the formal treaty was intended to be binding on other powers, and both were in fact repudiated. Kabas journey of North America in 1497 was England's immediate reply to the partition. Francis I of France voiced his celebrated protest:" **The sun shines for me as for others. I would very much like to see the clause in Adam's will that excludes me from a share of the world.** "King of Denmark refused to accept the pope's ruling, as far as the East Indies was concerned, Sir William Cecil, the famous Elizabethan statesman, denied the pope's right to "give and take King's Kingdom to whomever he pleases."* (Capitalism and Slavery, Pages 3 and 4.)

The first English slave trading expedition was that of Sir John Hawkins. In 1562 like so many Elizabethan ventures, it was a buccaneering expedition encroaching on the papal arbitration of 1493, which made Africa a Portuguese monopoly. The slaves obtained were sold to Spaniards in the West Indies. The English slave trade remain desultory and perfunctory in character until the establishment of British colonies in the Caribbeans and the introduction of the sugar industry when by 1660, the political and social upheavals of the Civil War period came to an end. England was ready to embark wholeheartedly on a branch of commerce whose importance to her sugar and her tobacco colonies in the New World was beginning to be fully appreciated. In accordance with the economic policies of the Stewart Monarchy, the slave trade was entrusted to a monopolistic company, the Company of Royal Adventurers Trading to Africa Incorporated in 1663 for a period of 1000 years. The Earl of Clarendon voiced the enthusiasm current at the time. "That the company would be founded a model equally to advance the trade of England with that of any other company, even that of the East Indies". The optimistic prediction was not realized, largely because of losses and dislocation caused by war with the Dutch, and in 1672 a new company, the Royal African Company, was created.

The policy of monopoly, however, remained unchanged and pro- voked determined resistance in two quarters. The merchants in the output ports struggled to break down the monopoly of the capital. (Capitalism and Slavery, pages 30 and 31.)

As Merivale wrote: **Slave Labor is dearer than free wherever abun- dance of free labor can be procured.**

This temporary service at the outset denoted no inferiority or degradation of the servants where Manorial tenants fleeing from the irksome restrictions, of feudalism Irishmen seeking freedom from the oppression of landlords and bishops.

In the transportation of felons, a whole hierarchy, from courtly secretaries and grave judges down to the jailers and turnkeys insisted on having a share in the spoils. Leading merchants and public officials were all involved in the practice:

Sir, Mr. Mayor, you, I mean kidnapper and an old Justice of the peace on the bench, I doe. Not know him and Old knave: He goes to the Tavern, and for a pint of sack he will bind people, servants to the Indies at the Tavern. A kidnapping knave. I will have his ears off before I go forth of town....... Kidnapper you, I mean, Sir... If it were not in respect of the sword which Is over my head. I would send you to Newgate You kidnapping, knave you are Worse than a pickpocket who stands there! I hear the trade of kidnapping is of great request. They can discharge a felon or a trader, provided they will go to Mr. Alderman's Plantation at the West Indies. (Capitalism and Slavery, pages 7, 10, 14 and 15.)

Now from the statements above made from the book of Capital- ism and Slavery, you can see the dissent amongst the kings of that day from. The actual agreement of 1493 and this gave birth to the whole era of piracy that began between the Europeans at sea. For those that felt they were left out of Adam's will, they decided to implore their actual navy on the high sea to rob those that weren't. This is nothing but a reflection of what they have always done to each other with warring with each other, colonizing and robbing each other. That's where the term or name in some cases Baron comes from: Robber Baron.

It was here that 400 years ago a force was built by Englishmen. Used by other Englishmen as their chattels or slaves. (White Cargo, page 33.)

Now, without further ado, allow me to introduce you to Lord Chief Justice. Sir John Popham.

*Before he occupied one of the great legal offices of state. John Poppin had been a highwayman and, according to one rumor, **probably a garrotter**," too.*

Popham was born in 1531 into an affluent Somerset family. He read law at Balliol College, Oxford, and in his 20s he was called to the bar and respectably married. Even then, however, he was exhibiting a different side to his character. He was a heavy drinker and a gambler and according to Lord Campbell, either to supply his profligate expenditure or to show his spirit.

Popham frequently sailed forth at night from a hostel in Southwark with a band of desperate characters and a planting themselves in Ambush on shooters heel or taking other positions favorable for attack and escape. They stopped travelers and took from them not only their money but any valuables, commodities they carried with them, boasting that they were always civil and generous, and that to avoid serious consequences they went in such numbers as to render resistance impossible.

Popham antics continued right through his twenties. Amazingly, he was never caught in his thirties. He decided he could make as much money from law as from highway robbery and developed an extensive practice in northwest England that brought him to the attention of the queen. With the queen rare ability to pick ruthless talent that could be used one day. Queen Elizabeth arranged a seat in Parliament for him, the former highwayman became Speaker of the House, then attorney general and finally Lord Chief Justice. He was a hanging judge, says Campbell. Ordinary larcenies and above all, in highway robbery, there was little chance of acquittal. It was the same with those who did not fit the Protestants orthodoxies the crown was trying to mold. Sir John pursued outspoken Puritans and Catholic priests to the scaffold. Under him hundreds of Jesuits and suspected sympathizers were sent to Turbine and Smithfield to be hanged, drawn and quartered, or if a woman, perhaps to be crushed to death or strangled before being burnt at the stake. When it came to the rich, Sir John could be lenient if the price was right. There was no more corrupt AIDS than the Elizabethan and the future Lord Chief Justice proved himself as buyable as any. (White Cargo; P.37-38)

The Magna Carta birth, the Inns of Court. These agents of chaos were released upon this New World. As we continue to go forth, you will see that this world was created on paper with a legal philosophy, and it was forced into reality. Nothing more than a fiction being made real by similar characters to Chief Lord Justice here that we are describing, but we will not stop here, you will see more.

Gorges wanted Popham's help in his American venture and present-ed the Lord Chief Justice with two of his Native Americans. The two men were soon partners and they aimed to bring together burghers from London and Plymouth, the members of the Gentry who had previ-ously invested in expeditions. On top of this list there would have been great merchants like Smythe and Aristocrats like Henry Wrottesley, the brilliant Earl of Southampton, who was William Shakespeare's patron. Most of the lobbying appeared to have taken place in the vast new banquet halls of the **Middle Temple,** Under the coats of arms of two door Knights that still hang there today over the heads of other ambitious lawyers.

In the winter of 1605-06, Popham approached the attorney General Sir Edward Coke. He laid the emphasis. Step on the riches to be had in America, but on England's desperate need for a dumping ground for criminals, Coke reported their conversation:

My Lord Chief Justice foresaw in the experience of his place the infinite numbers of cashiered captains and soldiers of poor artisans that would and cannot work and of idle vagrants that may and will not work, whose increase threatens the state, is affectionately bent to the plantations of Virginia.

More talk followed, with a great deal of haggling over who was to be in control. Eventually, the Virginia company was chartered with two divisions: A London company and a Plymouth company. The charter helped to give birth to a myth. Ostensibly, it was a remarkable document from a king who espoused the divine right to rule and conceded no powers without a struggle and a section on how the colonies were to be governed, James stated.

"I do declare in order that my loving subjects in America shall forev-er enjoy the right to make all needful laws for their own government, provided only that they be consistent with the laws of England. (White Cargo, pages 40. And 41.)

John Popham, one of the most powerful men in the government of Queen Elizabeth I. Popham, was the first to put to the test Sir Humphrey Gilbert's proposal for colonizing America with the dreads of England. What Popham tried would one day be one of the most hated features of English rule in America; Ambitions buried at Fort Saint George were to live on and change the face of North America. The short-lived force began in August 1607. It was to be the cen-terpiece of a new colony. A charter issued the previous year by King James I, restated English's claims to Virginia the entire length of the

Eastern American seaboard from Canada to Florida and authorized the establishment of the two colonies. One, under the Aegis of Sir Thomas Smythe, was to be in the South between the 38th and 40th 1st parallels, the other under the guidance of the Lord Chief Justice. Sir John Popham was to be in the north of New England.

The board argued for a stock, a joint stock company that could take a long view and ride the kind of setbacks that had been the ruin of so many previous ventures. Joint stock companies were relatively new entities in which individuals own shares they could sell without reference to their fellow stockholders. These companies were opening and in far corners of the globe to English trade. So why not a joint stock company to fund the next big English push to colonize America? (White cargo. Pages 33 and 34.)

The forays to America were drawn up and two joint stock companies of Knights, gentlemen, merchants, and other adventurers created. For the purpose, the two principal aims were announced as bringing infidels and savages living in those parts to human civility and the mining of gold, silver and copper. Three of the Crowns leading counselors helped draft the documents: Robert Cecil Chief Secretary of State; Sir Edward Coke, Attorney General; And the fearsome Lord Chief Justice Sir John Popham.

Cecil emerged as principal patron of the company that allocated the Southern territories, lined roughly between what is now Florida and New York. It was composed of men drawing mainly from our City of London. The inevitability became known as the London Company and later the Virginia Company. The key post of treasurer of the company's equivalent to the managing director was taken by Sir Thomas Smithy. Sir John Popham was the principal investor in the second company, drawn from our cities of Bristol and Exeter and of our town of Plymouth, and allocated New England. It came to be known as The Plymouth Company. Popham was a man whose character was written in his face and in one portrait he appears a physical giant with a scarlet robe of the High Court clinching around his bulk, a heavy, ugly face, glaring out cold eyes, cunning and suspicious: the face of a calculating unstoppable bully. In his voluminous lives of the Chief Justice of England, Lord Campbell referred to the Portrait and adds decorously: I am afraid he would not appear to great vantage in a sketch of his normal qualities, which lease I do him an injustice I would not attempt.

Sir John was the man who had passed the death sentence on Sir William Releigh, telling him. It is best for a man not to seek to climb too high lest he fall. He had participated in the trial of Queen Mary of

Scots and condemned to death Guy Fawkes and hundreds more. The miracle was that he did not join them on the gallows himself. (White Cargo, page 36.)

I hope that you notice in the passages that were placed above that the buttress of America was established in legal documents under the ideas of corporations and joint stock corporations that were drawn up by individuals of these Inns of Court. It is clear by the creation of these companies, there was no honorable intent, and there was an interest in labor, and it did not matter from whence the labor became or where it came from, but these were drawn up. Under the guise of this fictitious law that was created by theory and that came out of the left side to create a right, all for the purpose of a form of taxation and profit that would be funneled through to the left side. The Inns of Court, if you go back in this book, you will see it was created by merchants, and you have seen the word, as I pointed out before, firms being loosely used oftentimes, and it appears as if all of these legal men that came out of The Temple of London where basically the henchman for all that would be created in this New World. Their job was to create a legal basis to do everything that they needed to do to establish franchise corporations and to monetize and create an economic system to support all forms of commerce while protecting those who have interests within the companies. All out of the idea of forms of monopolies. Where it appeared to me through the documentation of the 14th century out of the establishment of the philosophy of the document of 1302. The expanded version of what would include the rest of the world was based on servitude. We know that servitude consists of nothing but a description of slavery. In closing, let me proceed.

Merivale: **Slavery was an economic institution of the first importance. It had been the basis of the Greek economy and had built up the Roman Empire.**

White servitude was the historic basis upon which negros slaves were constructed. The felon drivers in the plantations became, without effort, slave drivers. **In significant numbers, writer Professor Phillips. The Africans were latecomers, fitted into a system already developed.**

Here then, is the origins of negros slavery. The reason was economic. Not racial; It had to do not with the color of the laborers, but the cheapness of the labor. As compared with Indians and white labor, negros slaves were eminently superior in each case writes, Bassett. (Capitalism and slavery. Page 19.)

Economic Fact: The colonies needed labor and resorted to negro labor because it was the cheapest and best. This was not a theory; it was a practical conclusion deduced from the personal experiences of the planter. He would have gone to the moon if necessary for labor. Africa was nearer than the moon, nearer than the most populous countries of India and China. But their turn was to come. (Capitalism and Slavery, page 20.)

However, black slavery emerged out of white servitude and was based upon it, as the African American writer Lerone Bennett Jr has observed:

When someone removes the cataracts of whiteness from our eyes, and when we look with unclouded vision on the bloody shadows of the American past, we will recognize for the first time that the African Americans who were so often second in freedom were also second in slavery. (White Cargo, pages 14.)

I can only pray that you have found this book informative. That was and is my only objective. I can't say what pushed me to write this book; I was just inspired heavily at some point to write it. My objective was to create something that was a quick read that would not take the reader a long time. But packed the book with a bunch of facts along a timeline that the reader could follow in hopes that they would look and see the different volumes of books that were used to point out these patterns. I wanted to place these patterns on the timeline so the reader could follow them, and it called for me to bring a lot of books together to do this. I've read so many books, but these are the ones that are most important, and I tried to be as detailed as possible by giving you the references that you could go and look and find for yourself. I had been struggling through the course of writing this book trying to figure out if I wanted to make a conclusion to the book, and I will be honest, I did want to write a conclusion at the end, but my spirit has led me or guided me against it. I don't want you, as the reader, to be consumed with my thoughts or my vision of what I've just laid out because that's not important. The most important thing is that you arrive at your own conclusion. So, I would like to bid Godspeed on your journey moving forward with this information, and I hope that you come to a point where you arrive at whatever conclusion suits you best based on the research.

You have done additional to what I've pointed out or maybe even to what has been given or offered within this book. My dream is to bring the human family together to stop being misguided by so many fictitious ideas and blaming things on each other and find a common humanity within each other. And to see that we have all been, in one form or another, exposed to a lot of shenanigans with the mixture of hoodwinking. But I pray throughout the maze that we have been going through that we're able to find each other again because, at one point, we did not know color, and color only existed, as stated above, as a reflection of greedy people. Exploiting us all. I saved this one passage right here that I'll place for last. It's like a paragraph, but I've taken it out of the **Capitalism and Slavery book by Eric Williams**. And I encourage any and everybody to purchase this book, as well as the book **White Cargo** being armed with the information that you have out of what I've just written. This small paragraph touched me in a different way because it allowed me to kind of pretty much understand the system that was created. Once they went into the New World the governmental structure was based on pretty much profit. And the laws that were created were based on maintaining slaves under different descriptions to remain productive. And I pretty much see, and the professor pretty much states that's what we're still experiencing to this day:

*Importation of Negro slave labor in the British Caribbean. A phase in the history of the plantation. In the words of **Professor Phillips, the plantation system was "less dependent upon slavery than slavery was upon it..... The plantation system formed, so to speak, the industrial and social fabric of government....... While slavery was a code of written laws enacted for that purpose."***